FORTUNES OF WAR

The West Midlands at the Time of Waterloo

Editors: Andrew Watts and Emma Tyler

Published by West Midlands History Limited
Minerva Mill Innovation Centre, Alcester, Warwickshire, UK.
© 2015 West Midlands History Limited.
© All images are copyright as credited.

ISBN: 978-1-905036-21-9

Cover image: © National Gallery of Victoria, Melbourne.
Caric Press Limited, Merthyr Tydfil, Wales.

CONTENTS

COVER STORY

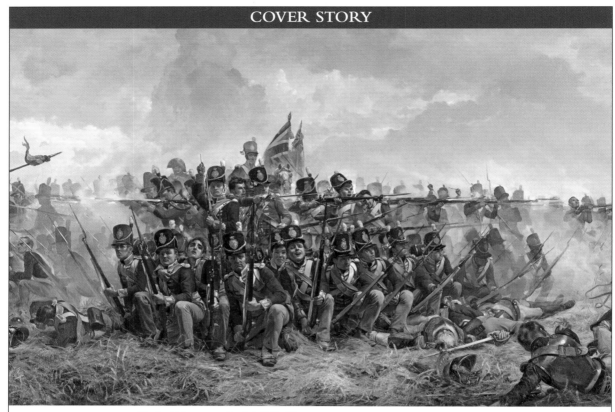

Elizabeth Thompson, English 1846-1933, *The 28th Regiment at Quatre Bras*, 1875.
Oil on canvas; 97.2 x 216.2 cm. National Gallery of Victoria, Melbourne. Purchased 1884 (detail).

The cover illustration shows a painting by Elizabeth Thompson, Lady Butler, dated 1875. It represents the 28th (North Gloucestershire) Regiment, which arrived as a reinforcement at Quatre Bras, situated between Brussels and Charleroi, on the eve of the Battle of Waterloo. Lady Butler selected a moment at about 5 o'clock in the afternoon, showing the courageous British square formation repelling, with laughter, a last charge from the French Cuirassiers and Polish Lancers, under Marshal Ney.

As a child, Lady Butler had been conducted over the field of Waterloo by an old campaigner. For the episode of Quatre Bras, she consulted *The History of the War in France and Belgium, in 1815*, by Colonel William Siborne (London, 1844). She made detailed preparations in England for the canvas and carried out life-size oil studies of hands 'to be very strong points, gripping brown besses'. In 1874 Colonel Browne arranged for her to sketch 300 Royal Engineers in full dress, at Chatham. They formed a four-deep square and fired in sections for her. She purchased a rye field at Henley-on-Thames, which children helped her to trample down. A Waterloo uniform was made for her at the Government clothing factory at Pimlico.

The painting attracted huge crowds on Studio Day at the Royal Academy, Millais among them. It was applauded at the RA banquet and praised by Ruskin in his Academy Notes. Lady Butler recorded in her diary: 'It seems to be discussed from every point of view in a way not usual with battle pieces. But that is as it should be, for I hope my military pictures will have moral and artistic qualities not generally thought necessary to military genre.' The immediacy of the moment expressed in *Quatre Bras* influenced late nineteenth-century British battle painting, when 'The Last Stand of the Regiment' became a common subject.

Annette Dixon, National Gallery of Victoria, Melbourne.

See Elizabeth Thompson's entry in the *Oxford Dictionary of National Biography* at www.odnb.com, freely accessible online with your public library card.

INTRODUCTION
Fortunes of War

Portrait of Arthur Wellesley (1769-1852), 1st Duke of Wellington.
Sir Thomas Lawrence, 1814.

In June 1815 the allied armies under the command of the Duke of Wellington finally defeated Napoleon at the Battle of Waterloo. Wellington's victory had a profound impact on European history, bringing to an end over a decade of war with France, and heralding the collapse of an imperial dynasty across the continent.

However, the Napoleonic Wars also touched the lives of millions of ordinary people, and continued to do so for years after Waterloo. In this special publication from **History West Midlands**, eleven leading writers and historians explore how the lives and fortunes of many West Midlanders were affected, both for the better and the worse, by Napoleon's relentless empire-building.

Fortunes of War reveals the West Midlands at a fascinating point in its history, as local industrialists grew rich on the proceeds of the gun trade, and families waited anxiously for news of loved ones who had gone to war. This new research also tells some of the little-known stories about this period, most notably that of Napoleon's brother, Lucien Bonaparte, whose own fluctuating fortunes of war saw him exiled from France before he took up residence in Worcestershire.

This book was conceived primarily to mark the bicentenary of the Battle of Waterloo in 2015. However, it also reflects our longstanding interest in the Napoleonic period and the historical links between France and the West Midlands. The strength of these connections became obvious to Emma Tyler in her former career as a genealogist, during which time she researched the history of Thorngrove House, the residence which belonged temporarily to Napoleon's younger brother Lucien. The Napoleonic Empire has also proved an enduring source of fascination for Andrew Watts in his research on nineteenth-century French writers such as Victor Hugo, who tried to make sense of Napoleon's defeat at Waterloo in *Les Misérables*. The experience of editing *Fortunes of War* has enabled us to explore new aspects of our passion for Napoleonic history and culture from a uniquely regional perspective.

The first part of this book focuses on the West Midlands between 1810 and 1815, and on the ways in which the ongoing war with France affected the social, economic and political life of the region. This was a period in which Birmingham became an important centre for the production of weapons, as local manufacturers supplied many of the guns and swords that Wellington's men carried onto the battlefield. The gun industry in particular helped to transform Birmingham into a global economic centre, but also provoked conflict and tension at home, not least with influential communities such as the Quakers, who found the profits made from war incompatible with their own pacifist beliefs.

Alongside its discussion of the Birmingham arms trade, the first part of the book also examines the role played by West Midlands soldiers in the Battle of Waterloo itself. Wellington's army included numerous local men, from rank-and-file soldiers to senior officers such as Field Marshal Henry Paget and General Rowland Hill, whose actions at Waterloo confirmed their status as legends of the Napoleonic Wars.

The experiences of these combatants are, however, only part of the story. One of our aims in this book is to show that Waterloo was not simply an end-point in West Midlands history, but that its impact has continued to resonate through the years. The second part of the book explores the immediate aftermath of the battle, and the ways in which Wellington's victory was reported in the local press, which delighted in recounting tales of the valour shown by local men on the battlefield.

In addition to considering how news of Waterloo was received in the West Midlands, we take up the story of Napoleon's exile on the distant island of St Helena, where he was guarded by the 53rd (Shropshire) Regiment of Foot. Finally, we reflect on the remembrance of Waterloo across the region, in the form of commemorative pottery produced in Stoke-on-Trent during the nineteenth and twentieth century, and through the monuments, street names, and other physical reminders of the battle which remain part of the West Midlands landscape today.

For people who wish to explore the Battle of Waterloo in their own way, the book provides information on places to visit across the region. Many of these locations – including the Queen's Own Hussars Museum in Warwick, the Birmingham Gun-Barrel Proof House, and Lord Hill's Column in Shrewsbury – are accessible to the public. We also invite readers to visit the website of the National Army Museum (www.nam.ac.uk), which contains numerous images of artefacts relevant to the battle, and

Napoleon (1769-1821) after his Abdication. Hippolyte (Paul) Delaroche, 1840.

© Napoleon (1769-1821) after his Abdication (oil on canvas), Delaroche, Hippolyte (Paul) (1797-1856)/Musée de l'Armée, Paris, France/Bridgeman Images.

the Waterloo 200 website (www.waterloo200.org) for educational resources and details of bicentennial events.

We would like to express our sincere thanks to Mike Gibbs, Malcolm Dick, and colleagues at **History West Midlands** for recognising the value of a book on the West Midlands and Waterloo. Special thanks are reserved for Elaine Mitchell, who guided this project expertly through every stage towards publication. Without doubt, her support proved the greatest of these fortunes of war.

Andrew Watts and Emma Tyler
April 2015

TIMELINE
1815: The Road to Waterloo

26 February: Napoleon escapes from Elba, where he has been exiled since April 1814 under the terms of the Treaty of Fontainebleau. He lands near Antibes on the French mainland on 1 March.

7 March: Napoleon's advance on Paris is halted temporarily by the French 5th Regiment, which engages his small force of men near Grenoble. Napoleon invites the opposing troops to kill him, but they respond with cries of 'Vive l'Empéreur!'

13 March: The Congress of Vienna declares Napoleon an outlaw.

19 March: Louis XVIII flees to Ghent after the garrison stationed on the outskirts of Paris defects to Napoleon.

20 March: Napoleon arrives in Paris, marking the beginning of his Hundred Days back in power.

25 March: Austria, Great Britain, Prussia, and Russia agree to mobilise 600,000 soldiers in order to put an end to Napoleon's ambitions once and for all.

10 June: Leading a force of some 124,000 men, Napoleon sets out from Paris intent on launching a pre-emptive strike on the armies of the Seventh Coalition.

15 June: Napoleon's army crosses the Belgian border near Charleroi and quickly secures a position between the armies of the Duke of Wellington and Field Marshal Blücher.

In the evening, Wellington attends a ball held in Brussels by the Duchess of Richmond, where he later receives word of Napoleon's advance.

16 June: Napoleon defeats the Prussians at the Battle of Ligny – his last victory on the battlefield. Wellington engages French forces under Marshal Ney at the crossroads of Quatre Bras, but without Prussian reinforcements, decides to withdraw his men to a position south of the village of Waterloo.

17 June: Napoleon joins Ney with the intention of attacking the British at Quatre Bras, but arrives too late to intercept Wellington's army.

18 June: The armies of the Seventh Coalition defeat Napoleon at Waterloo. Around 15,000 allied troops and a further 7,000 Prussians are killed or wounded; French casualties number around 25,000. Wellington declares the victory 'the nearest-run thing you ever saw in your life'.

19 June: Wellington gives news of the victory in a despatch to Lord Bathurst, Secretary of State for War and the Colonies.

21 June: The Waterloo Despatch arrives in London, and is published in *The London Gazette Extraordinary* the next day.

22 June: Napoleon abdicates for the second time.

3 July: Blücher defeats Marshal Davout, the French Minister of War, at Issy, in what would prove to be the final battle of the Napoleonic Wars.

15 July: After contemplating an escape to North America via the French Atlantic port of Rochefort, Napoleon surrenders to the British on board HMS *Bellerophon*.

20 November: Signing of the Treaty of Paris. Louis XVIII is returned officially to the French throne.

Andrew Watts and Emma Tyler

THE WEST MIDLANDS IN WAR AND PEACE

Malcolm Dick

The French Wars (1793-1815) influenced life in the region, but the impact of the conflict was not total. Births, deaths and daily existence continued often unaffected by the struggle. Moreover, industrialisation, agricultural improvement and urbanisation preceded and succeeded the conflict, but war and peace influenced the economy, shaped living standards and stimulated political activity.

© Shropshire Museums

Shropshire, where natural resources combined with scientific discovery to create a revolution.
The River Severn winds into the distance whilst flames and smoke pour from the blast furnaces in the gorge.
Afternoon View of Coalbrookdale 1777 by William Williams.

Across the Midlands, natural resources were harnessed for manufacturing. At Cromford in Derbyshire, Sir Richard Arkwright built the world's first successful water-powered cotton spinning mill.

The West Midlands was the silicon valley of the late eighteenth century. Pioneering iron-making in the Ironbridge Gorge, including new uses for the metal in bridge and building construction, ceramics in the Potteries, glassmaking in Stourbridge and chemicals in Tipton, married manufacturing with what we would now call scientific discovery. Carpet-making in Kidderminster, cotton manufacturing in the Derwent Valley and nail-making and coal mining in the Black Country, were other important industries, but less dependent on scientific knowledge.

The centre of West Midlands industry was the Birmingham area. This city of a thousand trades was renowned for its products before the outbreak of the French Wars. Matthew Boulton's Soho manufactory in Handsworth, which produced metalwares and the Boulton and Watt Soho Foundry in Smethwick, which made the parts for steam engines, were large factories by the early nineteenth century. They applied the division of labour, mass-production methods, precision engineering and mechanical power to making goods.

Most Birmingham industry was workshop-based, however, where manufacturers employed small numbers of workers in skilled and unskilled manual labour. The gun industry was an example, but printing, button making, japanning, wire drawing and brass making provided other instances. Birmingham had a complex

business structure, which produced a variety of goods for domestic and overseas markets.

James Bisset's *Directory* was a visual showcase of Birmingham industry during the war years. Published in two editions in 1800 and 1808, it contained a 'brief description of the different curiosities and manufactures of the place, accompanied with a magnificent directory, with the names and professions, &c. superbly engraved in emblematic plates'. The adverts provide a detailed and visually important record of the nature, extent and self-image of Birmingham manufacturers, including those who supplied the government with weapons of war, but the second edition coincided with a recession in the town.

A ruinous war

The French Wars were not kind to Birmingham. Its population may even have fallen in the 1790s, but, in any case, it failed to maintain the rapid rate of growth which had sustained it before that decade. From 1801 to 1811, its population rose from 73,670 to 85,755, a lower rate than in, for example, Manchester and Leeds.

The evidence for an economic recession is plentiful. In the fourth edition of his *History of Birmingham* (1809), William Hutton referred to: 'the ruinous war with France which has been the destruction of our commerce, caused 500 of our tradesmen to fail, stagnated currency, and thinned the inhabitants'. Unemployment was high and there are examples of businesses from japanning to wire manufacturing releasing labour.

Why was this? Exports were particularly important to Birmingham's prosperity. Between 1806 and 1812, Napoleon's continental system placed a trade embargo on France's enemies and therefore closed many European markets to Birmingham's manufacturers. The North American trade was also disrupted. To add to the problem, trade with the continent was forbidden by the British Government's Orders in Council in 1807. The 1812-1813 war with the USA had damaging commercial consequences. Taxation on incomes and property raised money for the government, but also reduced demand for goods. Bad harvests increased the price of bread.

The ending of war was also unkind. Birmingham's industries had to adjust to peace and manufacturers who supplied weaponry to the military, including gun and sword makers, were hit. Demobilised soldiers and sailors flooded the labour market. Wages fell and unemployment rose, thus putting pressure upon the local systems for poor relief. The Corn Law of 1815 introduced measures to prevent the import of foreign wheat and was widely condemned for keeping bread prices high at a time of pressures upon incomes.

A natural disaster compounded these man-made difficulties. In 1816, Tambora, the Indonesian volcano, erupted. Ash clouds were carried round the earth, blotting out the sun, and heavy frosts and rain ruined harvests and caused floods. Multiple economic problems provided the context for the radical activity in Birmingham which coincided with the ending of the war.

Political protest and unrest

Politically, the counties of the West Midlands were within the unreformed political system where the landed gentry and aristocracy dominated the political system. There were elections, but the franchise was based on a property qualification so that only a small number of men could vote. Constituencies were either county or urban ones. In the latter case, representation was confined to old-established towns and cities such as Warwick, Worcester, Shrewsbury and Lichfield.

Two of the largest and most rapidly growing towns in the country, Birmingham and Wolverhampton, were not able to elect their own Members of Parliament until after the passage of the Great Reform Act in 1832. Instead, voters in these towns elected their MPs as part of the county constituencies of Warwickshire and Staffordshire respectively.

Reproduced with kind permission of the Library of Birmingham.

'A brief description of the different curiosities and manufactures of the place'. James Bisset's *Directory* provides a visual showcase of Birmingham's manufactures in the early nineteenth century. Bisset's *Magnificent Guide or Grand Copperplate Directory for the Town of Birmingham,* 1808.

The West Midlands, nevertheless, was home to a tradition of reform. The best-known regional radical figure before the French Wars was Joseph Priestley (1733-1804) or 'Gunpowder Joe' as he was called by his conservative critics. Priestley advocated removing aristocratic privilege, breaking the link between the Anglican Church and the state and basing government upon the principle of the greatest happiness of the greatest number. The Priestley Riots of 1791 forced him to flee Birmingham and frightened fellow radicals. Following the outbreak of the French Wars in 1793, political reformers were accused of French Revolutionary sentiments and lack of patriotism. It was dangerous to want change.

Reform revived after 1812. In Birmingham, the banker Thomas Attwood (1783-1856) led a successful local and national campaign to repeal the Orders in Council. His success made him a national figure and in the immediate post-war years he campaigned to extend the vote and reform the House of Commons, culminating in the 1832 Reform Act. Attwood was middle-class, but his supporter George Edmonds (1788–1868) was from a humbler background. In the immediate post-war years, Edmonds helped to form Birmingham's Hampden Club to campaign for political reform. Major Cartwright (1740-1824), the veteran political reformer, saw the Midlands as fertile soil for seeding radical ideas. In 1816 he visited thirty-five Midland towns to speak at reform meetings.

In 1817, Edmonds' Hampden Club organised the first of Birmingham's mass political meetings. They were to prove highly effective in galvanising sentiment to pressure for political reform. The end of the French Wars coincided with the re-emergence of Birmingham's radical tradition.

Farming and landscape improvement

Most of the people in the West Midlands lived in rural areas where farming was the dominant economic activity and culture was more conservative than in towns like Birmingham. The high demand for bread during the French Wars increased the price of grain and stimulated wheat growing. This process was often accompanied by enclosure.

There were extensive regional and local variations. Oats were the main crop in the Staffordshire Moorlands and barley was produced in east Staffordshire, partly to serve the needs of the beer industry in Burton. Brewing was also served by hop growing in the Teme Valley and apples in Herefordshire were turned into cider. Market gardening was located around growing towns to provide vegetables and fruit to urban consumers. The Trent Valley specialised in cabbages, peas, carrots and potatoes and the Avon Valley in Worcestershire grew fruit.

The demand for horses multiplied during the French Wars. They were supplied to the military, but more importantly they were used for farm work, carting, hunting, mailcoaches, pit work and pulling canal boats. Horses were bred in Warwickshire, Derbyshire and Leicestershire and sold at horse fairs, the most important being in Rugeley in Staffordshire. One specialised centre for poultry was Meriden where Lord Aylsford raised turkeys for the London and Birmingham markets.

In 1812 the agricultural improver James Loch (1780-1855) became estate commissioner for the Marquis of Stafford, who owned vast estates in the West Midlands. In Shropshire, a county that had not been particularly renowned for its advanced agriculture, Loch encouraged investment in fertilisers, grains and livestock, drainage schemes, road building, tree planting and new brick-built farm buildings for milking, threshing and storage. Loch was an innovator who transformed much of the regional rural landscape.

Moving goods around the region

Transport was also improved, stimulated by agricultural, industrial and commercial activities. Road building and canal construction started before the French Wars, but following the outbreak of hostilities between Britain and France, another pioneering improver helped to transform the regional infrastructure.

Telford brought improvement to transport in the region, transforming the movement of goods. Here, he is pictured with an image of the Pontcysyllte cast-iron aqueduct.
Thomas Telford, FRS by Samuel Lane, c. 1822.

Thomas Telford (1757–1834) contributed significantly to the development of the region during this period. An architect and professional civil engineer, he built churches, including the remarkable St Mary Magdalen, Bridgnorth (1792-1795).

His canals and associated bridge building were his major claim to importance. The Longdon-on-Tern aqueduct on the Shrewsbury Canal (1795–6), and the Pontcysyllte aqueduct on the Ellesmere Canal (1805), used cast iron in construction. Sir Walter Scott described Pontcysyllte as 'the most impressive work of art he had ever seen'.

The Harecastle Tunnel, at Kidsgrove, Staffordshire on the Trent and Mersey Canal, was an engineering achievement, as was his Birmingham Canal improvement. This bypassed James Brindley's earlier meandering canal and created a huge cutting at Smethwick, which reduced the previous route by eight miles.

Reproduced with kind permission of the Library of Birmingham.

By the time of Waterloo, the sons and daughters of the Lunar men and women were taking their work forward. Maria Edgeworth, for example, was an active educationalist and author. *Portrait of Maria Edgeworth.*

In road building, Telford's main achievement was the London to Holyhead Road (now the A5), which was substantially improved in Shropshire and Staffordshire, but he also built iron bridges. An early example was Buildwas Bridge, Shropshire (1796), probably the second major iron bridge to be completed in Britain.

Religion in the region

The churches were the dominant cultural institutions. Most people's lives were regulated by the Church of England. In most localities, the parish church was the dominant building and the vicar or curate was the most important regulator of life. The sermon transmitted morality and laws to parishioners and managed the rites of passage of baptism, marriage and burial.

Roman Catholics were small in number as were Protestant dissenters. The latter, including Quakers, were minorities in Coventry and Birmingham. Unitarians and Baptists were important sects, also significant in Birmingham.

Methodism became strong during the war years in the Black Country and North Staffordshire.

Denominations were divided, but they united in their support for the abolition of the British slave trade which was secured in 1807. In Shropshire, the siblings Katherine Plymley (1758–1829) and Archdeacon Joseph Plymley (1759–1838) were at the centre of local campaigning. Anti-slave trade agitation mobilised local communities, involved women as well as men and provided a template for future pressure-group activities.

The Lunar Society and beyond

Not all cultural activity was religious. When the French Wars broke out, the Lunar Society, an influential regional network of intellectuals, was in decline. The Priestley Riots of 1791 were a major blow. The wars themselves dampened the effervescent cultural atmosphere which had flourished at Soho House and elsewhere. It became dangerous to question received ideas. Matthew Boulton, for one, emphasised his patriotism, by producing a medal, at his own cost, for each sailor who fought at Trafalgar in 1805.

When Waterloo was fought, several Lunar men (Matthew Boulton, Erasmus Darwin, Joseph Priestley and Josiah Wedgwood) were dead. Richard Lovell Edgeworth, Samuel Galton Jnr, James Keir and James Watt were alive, but they were old men. Initiatives passed to a younger generation of their sons, daughters and grandchildren. Maria Edgeworth was an active educationalist, James Watt Jnr and Matthew Robinson Boulton managed their fathers' businesses, the Darwins, Wedgwoods and Galtons contributed significantly to nineteenth-century manufacturing and intellectual life.

By 1815 it would have been misleading to describe the West Midlands as the silicon valley of Great Britain, but innovative science, economic and industrial expansion, radical protest and a culture of improvement were sustained.

Dr Malcolm Dick is Director of the Centre for West Midlands History, University of Birmingham and Editor-in-Chief, History West Midlands.

Further reading:
Eric Hopkins, *The Rise of the Manufacturing Town: Birmingham and the Industrial Revolution* (Sutton Publishing, 1998).
Peter M. Jones, *Industrial Enlightenment: Science, Technology and Culture in Birmingham and the West Midlands* 1760-1820 (Manchester University Press, 2008).
Marie Rowlands, *The West Midlands from AD 1000* (Part Four), (Longman, 1987).
Jenny Uglow, *In These Times: Living in Britain through Napoleon's Wars, 1793-1815* (Faber and Faber, 2014).
The *Oxford Dictionary of National Biography* contains biographies for many of the key figures mentioned in this article, and is freely accessible online with your public library card at www.odnb.com.
Many of the themes of this article are explored further on Revolutionary Players at www.revolutionaryplayers.org.uk.

THE GALTON FAMILY DURING THE NAPOLEONIC WARS

Jenny Uglow

Many of the guns used by British troops during the Napoleonic Wars were manufactured in Birmingham by the Galton family. The Galtons grew wealthy from the gun trade, but as the war with France intensified, their commercial prosperity set them on a collision course with the pacifist Quaker Society to which the family belonged.

When William Pitt declared war on France on a rainy night in February 1793, one of the first things the government needed was a good supply of guns. Over the next twenty-two years, until the final relief of Waterloo, these were supplied by Birmingham makers, including three generations of the Galton family, grandfather, father and son – Samuel, Samuel and Samuel.

The Galtons' firm was in Steelhouse Lane, near John Kettle's cementation furnaces, in an area where the back gardens of elegant Georgian houses had now become a maze of workshops. Samuel Galton senior (1720-1799) had entered the gun trade in the 1750s, making barrels and locks in the company run by his father-in-law, James Farmer. When Farmer's firm nearly crashed after the Lisbon earthquake in 1755, Galton bought him out, taking on a stream of government contracts. His son, Samuel Galton junior (1753-1832) – Samuel John to his family – joined the company at seventeen and when he was twenty-one his father put £10,000 into his business account and made him manager at Steelhouse Lane. A year later he was a partner and by the 1780s he had quadrupled his investment, and married

Reproduced with kind permission of the Library of Birmingham.

Samuel Galton junior contributed to Birmingham's economic success and the Lunar Society's scientific knowledge, but his gunmaking business brought him into conflict with his fellow Quakers. *Samuel Galton, The Younger (1753-1832).* From *The Life, Letters and Labours of Francis Galton*, Vol. I, 1914, Karl Pearson.

the redoubtable Lucy, from a Scottish branch of the Barclay family. They went on to have five sons, Samuel Tertius (1783-1844), Theodore, Hubert, Ewen Cameron – named after Lucy's relative, a flamboyant highland chieftain – and the nature-loving John Howard, and three daughters Mary Anne, Sophia and Adele, growing up in a household of noise, music and books, in town in winter and on their estate at Great Barr in summer.

Samuel junior was bulky and serious, with heavy brows and a piercing glance. His daughter, Mary Anne Schimmelpenninck, remembered how he spent the mornings in business in Birmingham, 'but from about one o'clock, when he usually returned, he was chiefly engaged at home in intellectual pursuits; and of these he had an endless variety'. A great supporter of Joseph Priestley and a friend of Matthew Boulton and James Watt, he was a keen member of the Lunar Society, writing on optics, colour, canals and birds, and building up a fine library and collection of scientific instruments.

The direct gaze of the 'redoubtable' Lucy Galton, Samuel junior's wife, a member of the Scottish branch of the Barclay family.
Mrs Samuel Galton (Lucy Barclay) (1757-1815).
From *The Life, Letters and Labours of Francis Galton,* Vol. 1, 1914, Karl Pearson.

Conflict with the Quakers

In 1793 when the first war orders arrived, the gunsmiths' district rattled with business, making muskets, carbines and pistols, and sending gun barrels and locks to London to be 'set up' at the Tower. The Galtons worked on larger and larger orders, including an unusual request for 5,100 expensive 'French pattern' muskets. In the crisis, gunmakers were asked to send in anything they could make, and they flooded the Tower with cheap guns of all shapes and sizes, until the Ordnance adopted the East India Company's standard firearm, a version of the 'Brown Bess' muzzle-loading flintlock known as the India pattern, cajoling the Birmingham makers to make these by giving them a higher payment for longer credit.

Galton was raking in money, but his gunmaking put him in a difficult position. He and Lucy belonged to old Quaker families, related to the Darbys, Gurneys, Lloyds and other powerful clans - and the

Quakers were pacifists. Before the war, at the Yearly Meeting in 1790 the Birmingham Meeting had issued a firm statement:

> *If any be concerned in fabricating, or selling Instruments of War, let them be treated with in love; and if by this unreclaimed, let them be further dealt with as those we cannot own. And we intreat that when warlike preparations are making, Friends be watchful lest any be drawn into loans, arming, or letting out their Ships, or Vessels, or otherwise promoting the destruction of the human Species.*

In 1795, accused of 'fabricating, and selling Instruments of War', the Galtons, father and son, were formally investigated by the Meeting and threatened with 'disownment'. Furious, Samuel junior pointed out that the family had made guns for seventy years without any rebuke. This did not necessarily imply an approval of war: indeed guns were vital for defence and for keeping the peace. He would give no pledge about abandoning the business, but would, he said, 'reserve to myself, a perfect Independence on that head'.

But the difficulty went further. The Galtons not only sold guns to the army, but to Africa traders, to exchange for slaves. This was anathema to the Quakers, who were leaders of the anti-slavery movement. Indeed, the Galton family themselves embraced the cause. The great campaigner Thomas Clarkson often visited Duddeston, the home of Samuel Galton senior. Of these visits to her grandfather, Mary Anne remembered:

> *In the evenings we often read pamphlets on the subject, or examined in detail the prints of slave ships and slave treatment, and both my cousins and I resolved to leave off sugar, as the only produce of slave labour within our province to discontinue.*

When this issue was raised, Samuel junior retorted that as far as his guns went, he could not be held responsible for their abuse:

> *Is the Farmer who sows Barley, – the Brewer who makes it into Beverage, – the Merchant who imports Rum, or the Distiller who makes Spirits; – are they responsible for the Intemperance, the Disease, the Vice, and Misery, which may ensue from their Abuse?' Why should he be held more responsible than those who traded in tobacco, rum, sugar, rice and cotton?*

The words carried a sting, as many Quakers were connected to the West India trades. But on 10 August 1796, Galton was disowned by the Society of Friends. Although Samuel Galton senior now retired at the age of 76, Samuel John continued defiantly.

Profiting from war

The war profits grew, reaching £139,000 in 1799 (around £7 million today). During the short-lived Peace of Amiens of 1802–1803, Galton became an arms supplier to the East India Company, thanks to Matthew Boulton's contacts, but he was happy to see war come again. When government officials asked Boulton what the weekly output of muskets and bayonets might be if every possible man in Birmingham was pressed into making them, Galton helped him work out an estimate. The gunmakers increased production to fourteen thousand muskets a week and the Ordnance agreed new terms and prices. As well as the faithful India pattern muskets Galton now had to cope with making the new rifles, recently adopted by the army: in 1806, when a huge order came in, Galtons sent 1,597 rifles, plus 15,106 rifle barrels and 11,980 locks, to be set up in London.

The firm increased investment and joined other gunmakers in a contractors' cartel, the Committee of the Manufacturers of Arms and Materials for Arms, which met at the Stork Hotel, Old Square, to set prices, deal with negotiations with the Ordnance, and amend the apprenticeship rules so that more men could be trained in each workshop. But by now Samuel Galton junior had had enough.

At fifty, he was a wealthy man, making money from canal shares, rents and investments in Welsh copper smelting as well as guns. In 1804 he set up as a banker, handing the gunmaking over to his eldest son, Samuel Tertius – the third Samuel. Three years later Tertius married Violetta, the lively daughter of his father's old Lunar Society friend, Erasmus Darwin: their youngest son Francis would become a well-known eugenicist – though not as famous as his cousin, Charles Darwin.

A life of leisure

The Galtons were now leisured and wealthy, going to Bath for their health and to London to shop, see exhibitions and catch the latest plays. While Mary Anne remained deeply religious, her sisters Adele and Sophia enjoyed gossip and fashions. The whole family followed the war news eagerly – after Trafalgar the sons wrote splendid gossip in mock naval language. They suffered their own tragedy in the death of Tertius's brother Theodore from fever in 1810, on his way home from a tour of Spain, Turkey and Greece, in defiance of the war, with his brother-in-law Sacheverel Darwin. 'They mean to pay their respects to the Knights at

Reproduced with kind permission of Frank James.

Samuel Tertius Galton, eldest son of Samuel junior and Lucy, wound up the gunmaking business after Waterloo, ending the dilemmas the business could bring.

Malta – & to Mt Aetna in Sicily. But a little more formidable mountain is, I fear, in the way – it is Bonaparte!' wrote his mother Lucy. But the Galtons also saw how people's lives were troubled by wartime hunger, trade restrictions and industrial unrest. And by 1812, although muskets by the thousand were being shipped to Wellington's armies in the Iberian Peninsula, Tertius began to work for peace. With fellow manufacturer Joseph Webster, he formed a committee to promote a peace petition and correspond with the Quakers in other towns. War, these petitions pointed out, was destructive of human happiness and all the best interests of mankind, 'the crime of corrupt humanity'.

In 1815, after Waterloo, Tertius was among the men who took addresses from Birmingham to congratulate the Prince Regent on the restoration of peace, and when the wartime orders ceased, he gave up gunmaking altogether. Ten years later, after the financial crisis of 1825, Tertius slowly wound up the Galton bank, finally closing it in 1831. Over the past decades, the Galton family had played a central part in the great story of Birmingham's growth, illustrating both the riches, and the dilemmas, that gunmaking could bring.

Jenny Uglow's latest book is *In These Times: Living in Britain through Napoleon's Wars, 1793-1815* (Faber & Faber, 2014). She is a biographer and historian, author of *The Lunar Men: The Friends who Made the Future* (Faber & Faber, 2003).

Further reading:
De Witt Bailey and Douglas A. Nie, *English Gunmakers. The Birmingham and Provincial Gun Trade in the 18th and 19th Century* (Arms and Armour Press, 1978).

John Cookson, *The British Armed Nation*, 1793-1815 (Oxford University Press, 1997).

Christina C. Hankin (ed.), *The Life of Mary Anne Schimmelpenninck*, (Longman, Brown, Green, Longman, and Roberts, 1858).

Karl Pearson, *The Life, Letters and Labours of Francis Galton*, 3 Vols. (1914–30), Vol. I (Cambridge University Press, 1914).

The Galton archives. Letters from four generations of the Galton family, from 1741-1882, are held in Archives & Heritage at the The Library of Birmingham, MS 3101/C/D.

Revolutionary Players at www.revolutionaryplayers.org.uk includes much information on Samuel Galton junior and his work, interests and connections.

A BROTHER IN EXILE: LUCIEN BONAPARTE IN THE WEST MIDLANDS

Emma Tyler

Between 1811 and 1814 the Midlands played host to a surprising visitor when Napoleon's brother Lucien was detained as a prisoner of war en route to voluntary exile in America. After six months in Ludlow, Lucien bought Thorngrove in Worcestershire, where he lived with his family and an extensive retinue.

© Mary Evans/Tallandier

An unexpected visitor to Worcestershire. Lucien Bonaparte, brother of Napoleon, was detained as a prisoner of war in the county. He remained there under parole from 1811 until his brother, the Emperor, abdicated in 1814.
Portrait of Lucien Bonaparte by François Xavier Fabre.

In January 1811 Lucien Bonaparte (1775-1840), the man whom Walter Scott would describe eighteen years later as the ablest of Napoleon's brothers, arrived in the Midlands. He and his family had set sail from Rome in August 1810, en route to voluntary exile in America. Napoleon owed to Lucien the success of his coup d'état of November 1799 (18 Brumaire in the Republican calendar), which drew the Revolution to a close and established Napoleon as First Consul. However, an increasingly fractious relationship over Napoleon's imperialist tendencies had deteriorated to the point of rupture some months previously: the 1811 imperial almanac omits Lucien from the list of the Emperor's brothers.

The British, fearing that Lucien would become involved in a plot on American soil, had intercepted his ship off the Sardinian coast. After a two-month detention in Valletta, he was conveyed to England as a prisoner of war under parole, along with a forty-strong entourage: his wife, seven children (including two by his first wife Christine Boyer and his wife's daughter from a previous marriage), his nephew, his secretary, a doctor, chaplain, tutor and painter, and twenty-three Corsican and Italian servants. The whole entourage landed at Plymouth in December 1810. Despite the circumstances, relations were more than cordial. Lucien presented the Captain with a diamond watch and received in return a double-barrelled shot-gun, which became his hunting weapon of choice while in England.

Lucien Bonaparte's forty-strong party at Thorngrove House included his second wife, seven of his children, and his nephew. This family portrait was commissioned by *Mme* Bonaparte in 1815, a year after the family left Worcestershire.
Portrait of the Family of Lucien Bonaparte by Jean-August-Dominique Ingres, 1815.

Prisoner of war in Ludlow

After 22 weeks of travelling, Lucien and his family, along with 33 tons of baggage, arrived at Dinham House in Ludlow, the occasional town residence of Lord Powis (the son of Clive of India). This was only intended as a temporary measure: he had been due to go to Lymore Hall, another of Lord Powis' residences. This was in Montgomery, one of Britain's 50 'parole towns'; several French officers already housed there had been moved out in preparation for Lucien's arrival, but at the last moment the house was deemed to be in too much of a state of disrepair.

The Bonapartes stayed in Shropshire for six months, hosting concerts and lavish dinner parties and drawing tourists into the town. Yet the local population was at best ambivalent towards its new celebrity guests. Kidderminster Library holds a collection of manuscript notes extracted from the voluminous diaries of Katherine Plymley (1758-1829) of Longnor, which record the following incident:

> At a ball at Ludlow he gives his arm to Lady Powis - Mr Bather remarks 'this fellow thrusts out his republican elbow to an English Countess of one of the 1st families & she condescends to take it & is to consider it an honor.'

There were more public expressions of disapproval: stones were thrown at Lucien's children, and there were altercations between two of his servants and some of the townspeople.

THE PAROLE TOWNS OF THE WEST MIDLANDS

In eighteenth-century Europe it had been common practice for countries in conflict to exchange prisoners of war of equivalent rank, using vessels known as cartel ships. Officers were commonly released under oath not to fight again. This system largely broke down during the Napoleonic era, partly as a result of a 1793 decree that French officers should not honour their parole, their Republican duty outweighing their duty as a gentleman.

Consequently, the decade of the Napoleonic Wars saw a huge increase in the number of French prisoners of war held in Britain. They were housed in existing prisons such as Portchester or Norman Cross, new buildings such as Dartmoor, or held in squalid conditions in hulks off the southern coast.

Approximately 4000 officers were permitted to live under parole, in receipt of a small allowance from the British government, in one of fifty designated towns. There were eight parole towns in the West Midlands, in Ashbourne and Chesterfield in Derbyshire, Bishop's Castle, Bridgnorth, Oswestry and Whitchurch in Shropshire, and Leek and Lichfield in Staffordshire.

Move to Thorngrove

After a lengthy search, and not before he had beseeched the Prince of Wales for permission to proceed to America, Lucien placed himself at a greater remove from local attentions. He acquired Thorngrove in the parish of Grimley in Worcestershire. What was once a motley jumble of meadows, pastures and assorted buildings had been transformed two decades previously, by an ambitious young man, William Cross, into a 130-acre country estate with a mansion house fitted with hot and cold baths, stables, coach houses, hop kilns and a pleasure ground with a lake and ornamental lawns. The brewing enthusiast had fallen into bankruptcy following an unwise investment. Lucien purchased Thorngrove for £13,500 from its subsequent owner, John Lagier Lamotte, a former trader in the East Indies, whose parents had fled to London in the wake of France's persecution of Huguenots.

With Lucien at Thorngrove House were his second wife, Alexandrine Jouberthon (top), who created a comfortable and lively family home, and two of the children from his first marriage to Christine Boyer (bottom).

Life on the estate

At Thorngrove, Lucien lived the life of a country gentleman, applying for a licence to shoot game, and maintaining a large stable of horses. Under the supervision of Colonel Leighton, he enjoyed a four-mile range of parole, which included the city of Worcester. Leighton received Lucien's mail in a locked portfolio and vetted the contents before passing it on.

Lucien lavished attention upon the estate, with the help of Thomas Knight, President of the Horticultural Society, whose acquaintance he had made while in Ludlow. The particulars of sale in 1814 would seem to indicate that he added 'graperies' and melon pits to the existing hothouses and walled gardens; he may also have stocked the lake with fish. He certainly commissioned the construction

of 'une jolie cabane', as his *Memoirs* record, a mile away from the main residence, to use as a writing retreat. He purchased 'a large commodious Pleasure Boat' to take out on the lake, and an elegant gig, lined in blue, with red Moroccan upholstery, and lamps. That part of his art collection that he had taken into exile was finally unpacked, including three works by Raphael and copper engravings by Fontana, Pistrucci (who was to become the Chief Medallist at the Royal Mint) and Carattoni.

The family led an impressive *train de vie*, extending lavish hospitality, much to the delight of the local shopkeepers. Liveried servants welcomed several prominent Whigs as houseguests, among them the Duke of Norfolk, the Marquess of Lansdowne and the future Lord Chancellor Lord Brougham, along with artists and academics from Oxford. Not all the visitors appreciated what they found. In a letter to her son in 1813, Melesina Trench reported that an acquaintance had seen Lucien 'Buonaparte' writing 'another epic in his observatory', but does not admire him.

An article reproduced in *The Times* in August 1811 gives us an insight into life on the estate:

> About a fortnight ago the whole family were employed in making hay before the house. They used nothing but their hands in throwing it about; and laughed at the English of the neighbourhood who have a different custom. LUCIEN appears to be always wrapped in thought and gloom; he moves gracefully to such people as salute him, but never speaks. The latter may be owing to his being almost ignorant of the English language. Madame is agreeable and chatty; and very particular in making the young part of her family observe the strictest politeness to strangers.

The county town of Worcester lay within the four-mile range of Lucien Bonaparte's parole. It was an important regional religious, cultural and economic centre. *Picturesque Views of the Severn*, Thomas Harral, 1824.

Madame Bonaparte

Madame had been the chief cause of the breakdown in relations between Lucien and his brother. Alexandrine Jouberthon (*née* de Bleschamps) had been of uncertain marital status when she married Lucien in 1803. Her husband had died in the French colony of Saint-Domingue, but no death certificate had arrived. Napoleon had urged Lucien to divorce her, had indeed passed a statute in 1806 declaring marriages of the imperial family to be 'null and void if contracted without the permission of the Emperor', and refused to acknowledge the succession rights of the children. Lucien had been offered his pick of European thrones in return for relinquishing her.

Alexandrine appears to have thrown herself into life at Thorngrove. She established a family home full of music and laughter. The house boasted 'a sweet-toned harpsichord', a guitar, and – quite a novelty in English society in 1814 – a four-pedalled French pianoforte and a barrel-organ. There was a billiard table and a library.

The family staged plays and held concerts. Alexandrine doted upon her young family and dressed them finely, much to the delight of the local newspapers (*plus ça change*): 'The youngest child has so much gilt and glitter in its dress, that in the sunshine it resembles an orb of moving fire.' In 1813, she gave birth to her son, Louis Lucien. The child's baptism is recorded in the Roman Catholic registers of Mawley Hall in Shropshire, the home of the Blount family, with whom the Bonapartes had forged a friendship whilst in Ludlow.

Managing such an extensive household of course brought its complications. In December 1811, *The Times* reported that *Madame* Lucien's governess had arrived in Plymouth, intending to return to Italy 'in consequence of ill health'. There were further reports of servants deserting, quarrelling violently or being banished from the premises. On its departure, the entourage had dwindled to half its original number. There were family troubles too: Alexandrine's younger stepdaughter Christine suffered from what Lucien's supervisor

17

Colonel Leighton described as 'a tendency to deformity', for which she occasionally received treatment while in England. This explains the presence, when the house was cleared, of 'two elegant mahogany reclining frames to correct deformities in the human body'.

Meanwhile, Alexandrine was pursuing ambitions of a literary career, writing a work in decasyllabic verse entitled *Bathilde, reine des Francs* (Bathild, Queen of the Franks). The thought of Lucien's wife achieving fame greatly exercised Napoleon, who took steps to prevent the publication of *Bathilde*, as the Duchesse d'Abrantès' memoirs record. In the summer of 1811, a mysterious visitor spent ten days with the household, claiming to be an admirer of *Mme* Lucien and her work. Thirty-six hours later, one *Mme* Simons-Candeille was commissioned by the Emperor to write a historical novel bearing the same title, using extensive notes provided by the spy. The work was published by the end of the year, putting an end to Alexandrine's ambitions.

Lucien's scholarly pursuits

Lucien pursued his own intellectual ambitions while at Thorngrove. He wrote a work on Etruscan art, and a tragedy called *Clotaire*, which was performed to owners of neighbouring properties. He developed an interest in astronomy, cultivating the acquaintance of William Herschel, from whom he ultimately purchased a ten-foot telescope. This explains why his writing retreat at Thorngrove is often referred to as an observatory. One of the more surprising visitors was a young Charles Babbage, who had met Lucien through his future bride, Georgiana Whitmore of Dudmaston Hall in Shropshire. Babbage's biographer, Anthony Hyman, attributes both Babbage's sense of style and his 'militant approach to science' to the acquaintanceship. Lucien shared his brother's belief in the ability of science to reform society, and his conversations with Babbage were influential in cementing the latter's drive to bring England into a new technological age, culminating in Babbage's invention of the difference and analytical engines, ancestors of today's computers.

Leaving England in secret

Lucien was liberated as the terms of Napoleon's abdication were being laid down. The *Memoirs* record that on the day of Napoleon's departure for Elba, Lucien's secretary arrived in Paris to request from Talleyrand safe-passage across France for his employer.

He met with a flat refusal, so Lucien's chaplain hatched a scheme: he obtained from the British a passport for himself and a 'secretary', and it was thus disguised that Lucien passed through France, arriving in Rome at the end of May.

The family followed on in August; Thorngrove was placed on the market and its contents sold off by the Birmingham auctioneers, Robins and Terry. The effects were described at length in the *Worcester Herald* and included approximately thirty bedsteads of varying types (rather exceeding the number of bedrooms), 'a great number of handsome Brussels and other floor, and bed-round carpets' and a full 650lbs of 'good, family cheese'. The auctioneers gave prominent place to a mangle, which perhaps seemed to them a rather new-fangled piece of equipment. They were most aggrieved, on arriving to conduct the sale, to discover that the horses had already been sold, and the 300 copies of the *Galerie de Lucien Bonaparte* (containing engravings of his paintings) sent to London.

Postscript

Throughout his stay in Worcestershire, Lucien had worked on his epic poem, *Charlemagne ou l'Église délivrée* (Charlemagne or The Church Delivered). Early reactions to the text were promising: Byron declared himself 'electrified' by a work which 'really surpasses anything beneath Tasso', and offers to translate it into English were plentiful. By the time of its publication, however, the intial enthusiasm had been stifled by Lucien's decision to reconcile with his brother after his escape from Elba. Consequently, sales were disappointing: Lucien had met, as the *Memoirs* put it, his poetic Waterloo in England.

Emma Tyler is Lecturer in French Studies at the University of Birmingham.

Further reading:

Francis Abell, *Prisoners of War in Britain*, 1756-1815 (Oxford University Press, 1914).

Gavin Daly, 'Napoleon's Lost Legions: French Prisoners of War in Britain, 1803–1814.' *History*, 89:295, 2004, pp.361-380.

Eileen Holt, *The Exile of Lucien Bonaparte 1810-1814*, a translation (1986). Available in the Worcestershire Archive.

Barney Rolfe-Smith, *A Gilded Cage: Lucien Bonaparte, Prisoner of War 1810-1814* (Stonebrook, 2012).

Notes by Mrs. Marie Corbett of Longnor from a voluminous diary by Miss K. Plymley, the sister of Archdeacon Owen (1924). The notes are bound and available at Kidderminster Library, in the Local Reference section.

THE RANK AND FILE

Andrew Bamford

Soldiering was a hard way of life in 1815. Despite this, men continued to enlist during the Napoleonic Wars in order to escape unemployment, see the world, and do their patriotic duty. Among these rank-and-file soldiers were men from the West Midlands, some as young as fifteen.

Recruiting sergeants' appeals to patriotism were hard to resist. The fluctuations of the agricultural year and economic hardship drove many to sign up. *He won't be a soldier.* Aquatint by Schutz after Rowlandson.

The names and careers of Wellington's generals are well-documented. For more junior officers, we at least have names and service histories, and not infrequently private letters as well. Trying to get a feel for the man in the ranks, however, is more complex, and not helped by misapplication of Wellington's much-quoted characterisation of them as the 'scum of the earth'. Even Wellington went on to say that service in the Army had made 'fine fellows' of unpromising material, and in fact the ranks of the British Army in 1815 contained men from a variety of walks of life, who had enlisted for all manner of reasons.

Understanding why men signed up is difficult. On the face of it, a soldier's life was hard, and military service carried an element of social stigma. Yet there were certainly those who signed up for patriotic motives, a sense of adventure, or a fancy for the military life. Of course, a recruiting sergeant's patter made the most of these elements, whilst downplaying the reality of hard marches and short rations that made up much of a soldier's life on campaign.

Military service had traditionally been a last resort for those unable to find work in civilian life, and the changes inherent in the Industrial Revolution meant that just as some trades thrived – Birmingham, for example, was a centre for the production of edged weapons, and did very well out of the increased wartime demand – others slumped.

Weavers were particularly hard hit, finding themselves replaced by mechanisation, and formed a sizeable proportion of recruits, whilst the cycles of the agricultural year helped ensure a steady stream of unemployed farm labourers seeking to don a red coat.

As the Napoleonic Wars progressed, however, more and more was also made of the militia regiments raised as a home defence force. Men were called up by ballot for militia duty, but efforts were then made to persuade those who proved to be good soldiers to transfer to the regular army. Already trained, militiamen became an increasingly important source of recruits as time went on, and almost all of the regiments that fought at Waterloo had topped up their ranks with militia drafts before embarking on campaign.

West Midlands soldiers at Waterloo

Finding West Midlanders who fought in the ranks at Waterloo is not straightforward. Many of Britain's infantry regiments – of which there were 104 in 1815 – had a county designation as well as their regimental number. Thus, the 6th and 24th

were assigned to Warwickshire, the 29th to Worcestershire, and the 38th and 64th to Staffordshire. None of these regiments fought at Waterloo, although some of them joined Wellington's command in time for the final advance on Paris.

Some of the county designations, however, had in many cases been only nominal when they were assigned back in the eighteenth century, and were even less relevant by 1815. Some counties – Derbyshire, for one – had no assigned regiment, and many regiments including the Foot Guards, the rifles, and the cavalry, had no assigned county. Almost without exception, English regiments had a large Irish contingent, as Ireland remained an excellent recruiting area.

A sample of Birmingham recruits from 1809 shows that out of 57 men who signed up, only five joined the local 6th Foot (1st Warwickshire), which in fact did most of its recruiting for that year in Manchester. On the other hand, no fewer than 31 Birmingham men joined the 32nd Foot (Cornwall), and another thirteen the 3rd Foot Guards (Scots Guards). The remainder were spread amongst the 1st Foot (Royal Scots), and the 8th Foot and 7th Hussars, neither of which had any territorial affiliation.

From this selection of regiments, only the 6th and 8th did not fight at Waterloo. Bearing in mind that this is just a single year's sample, it is inevitable that Wellington's army in 1815 contained a good proportion of men from the towns and villages of the West Midlands.

A recent study of the second battalion of the 69th Foot (South Lincolnshire), which fought at Quatre Bras and Waterloo, demonstrates this point. Amongst a rank-and-file strength drawn from across the British Isles, we find Private John Stokes of Kidderminster, aged only seventeen but already with two years' service under his belt, and Private Joseph Dale from Stone in Staffordshire. Stokes served for a further 21 years after Waterloo, but Dale was evidently not cut out for soldiering since he deserted less than year after the battle.

A young man's war

That so young a soldier as John Stokes fought at Waterloo may seem surprising, but in many ways much of Wellington's army was composed of inexperienced regiments containing many young recruits. Although

Little is known about many of the rank-and-file soldiers who fought at Waterloo but amongst their numbers were men from the towns and villages of the West Midlands. *Battle of Waterloo,* aquatint by W.T. Fry after Dighton.

most of the cavalry regiments were veteran units that had fought in the Peninsular War, much of Wellington's Peninsular infantry had, after the victory of 1814, been sent to help defend Canada from American invasion.

Although known as the War of 1812, the Anglo-American conflict did not end until early 1815, and many regiments were still on their way back to Europe when Waterloo was fought. The core of Wellington's infantry was drawn from an army that had been scraped together in late 1813 to help liberate the Netherlands, and which had remained in the Low Countries ever since, topped up with regiments of Peninsular veterans that had either never been sent to North America, or else had made it back to Europe in time.

Even the rawest battalions had a leavening of veterans. The third battalion of the 14th Foot (Buckinghamshire), raised only in 1814, was described by one general as a set of boys, and disparaged by more seasoned comrades as 'peasants' fresh from the plough. Yet in its ranks we find

veteran Private Thomas Williams from Newcastle-under-Lyme, aged 38 and a soldier for six years. Possibly the oldest man in the battalion, his experience nevertheless did not save him and he was one of fourteen men to lose their lives as the 14th helped hold the right flank of Wellington's line throughout the fighting at Waterloo.

Andrew Bamford is a military historian and the author of several books on the Napoleonic Wars, including *Sickness, Suffering and the Sword: The British Regiment on Campaign (1808-1815)* (University of Oklahoma Press, 2013).

Further reading:
Antony Brett-James, *Life in Wellington's Army* (Donovan, 1994).
Philip J. Haythornthwaite, *Redcoats: The British Soldiers of the Napoleonic Wars* (Pen & Sword, 2012).
Richard Holmes, *Redcoat. The British Soldier in the Age of Horse and Musket* (Harper Collins, 2001).
Sir Charles Oman, *Wellington's Army* 1809-1814 (Edward Arnold, 1913).
All of the soldiers who were awarded the campaign medal for taking part in the Battle of Waterloo, including many of the rank and file, are recorded in the Waterloo Medal Roll. More information about the document and the Medal can be found by entering 'Waterloo' into the search box of the Royal Mint's Museum website at www.royalmintmuseum.org.uk.

BIRMINGHAM AND WELLINGTON'S MUSKETS

David Williams

The Birmingham gun trade was well established by the time the Napoleonic Wars broke out in 1803. Driven by technical innovators such as the Galton and Ketland families, the munitions industry helped to turn Birmingham and the Black Country into a global economic powerhouse which supplied weapons to the military – and for the slave trade.

During the Napoleonic Wars close to 750,000 men served in the British Army. At Waterloo, Wellington fielded an allied army of 67,000. Many of these were infantry men – the Foot – all of whom would have had access to gunpowder weapons and small arms. The Foot fought *en masse*, either in a two-deep 'thin red line' formation, or in a square when attacked by cavalry. Fighting was done at close quarters with volley firing of the musket and fixed-socket bayonet. Among the ranks, the cry 'give them the Brummagem' was often heard as the signal to go in with the bayonet.

The primary infantry weapon of the Napoleonic Wars was the India Pattern Brown Bess musket. This robust flintlock was adequate and significantly better suited to mass manufacture in wartime than the highly-finished earlier patterns of Brown Bess. Brown Bess was the affectionate name that British soldiers gave to their muskets. From the 1720s these smooth-bore weapons were made under the Ordnance System, which meant that they were essentially assembled and finished at the Tower of London from components supplied by the London and Birmingham makers. The first India Patterns had been diverted to the British Army from the stores of the East India Company and originally were made to the design of Colonel Windus, the Company's Inspector of Small Arms, in 1771. Supply and scale-up in war have always been a problem for the British. We rarely prepare for war at scale, and there was a crisis of supply when the French Wars re-ignited in 1793. The Birmingham suppliers responded and turned themselves into a manufacturing powerhouse.

Birmingham and Black Country guns

Birmingham had been supplying arms since before the English Civil War, though until the 1690s these were primarily edged weapons. During the creation of the standing army in the reign of William III, the Warwickshire MP Sir Richard Newdigate of Arbury Hall had noticed that there was an opportunity for his local craftsmen to supply the new flintlock muskets. The first contractors were led by Thomas Hadley of Halesowen. During the eighteenth century the country was more often at war than at peace,

During the Napoleonic Wars the India Pattern Brown Bess musket was the weapon of choice for the British infantry. This Birmingham-made gun was supplied by Ketland and Allport, one of the largest suppliers of India Patterns.

especially with Bourbon France and then post-revolutionary France, and this recurrent state of conflict exercised a dominant influence on economic development.

Fed by wartime demands, gunmaking grew as a technically advanced industry in Birmingham and the Black Country during the eighteenth century. Many of the barrels and locks manufactured during this period came from the Black Country, where the abundance of coal was a significant advantage in an industry dominated by metal working and forging. The American Wars from 1776 first engaged the trade in the supply of military rifles. The Midlands trade began to overtake that of London and the Low Countries, thus establishing the region as one of the global centres of the industry. West Midlands manufacturers supplied guns to the new colonies, especially the Americas, and the slave trade. The demand for weapons in the military, civilian and slave markets helped the regional gunmaking industry to grow prosperous and accumulate capital in much the same way as earlier Dutch munitions suppliers had done in the seventeenth century.

Key protagonists

Military locks were externally marked with the names of the maker until 1764, a fact which helps us to build a picture of the important manufacturers in this burgeoning industry. It is clear that many of the families became gunmaking dynasties, for example, the Quaker Farmer and Galton families who seem to have dominated much of the eighteenth-century trade.

A key figure in the local gunmaking business in the eighteenth and early nineteenth century was Thomas Ketland,

A classical monument celebrates some fifteen Birmingham gunmakers, including, Samuel Galton. The image presents a patriotic view of the industry. Bisset's *Magnificent Guide or Grand Copperplate Directory for the Town of Birmingham*, 1808.

who was born in 1737. Both the Galtons and the Ketlands had large-scale works and contributed to the subsequent growth of Birmingham in manufacturing, commerce and banking. Other prominent names in the industry during this period were the Willits, and the Edges. Benjamin Willits is notable for building a windmill, called 'Willits Folly' by the Wednesbury locals, to try to overcome the practical difficulty of a lack of water power. The trade concentrated in particular areas of Birmingham,

'For the service of His Majesty's Ordnance'. The flintlock of this 1809 Brown Bess Musket displays the Royal Cypher of George III.

It has been estimated that between 1804 and 1815 the Birmingham and Black Country trade made 1.75 million military weapons, 3 million military barrels and 2.9 million gunlocks, together with an estimated million guns for the East India Company and half a million sporting guns.

building near the new estate that became known as Old Square, where Joseph Farmer had his first forge in Bull Street in 1702. Gunmakers also set up premises in the new developments around the church of St Mary's, built in 1774. The church itself has long since disappeared, but the name by which this area is still commonly known – the Gun Quarter – serves as a lasting reminder of the trade that once flourished in this part of Birmingham.

Gunmaking methods

Importantly, the Birmingham trade was not constrained by the guild system, unlike London's, and so its approach was characterised by specialisation and the division of labour. Consequently, Birmingham's early industrial district grew up around small gunmaking workshops, rather than the large-scale factories to which the Industrial Revolution had given birth elsewhere.

Manufacturing processes were simple but specialised in exploiting the division of labour and used innovative hand tools.

Some processes needed mechanical power, for example, barrel grinding, and they were driven initially by water and latterly by steam. Most workshops were small, but the trade was organised and operated by factors who were sophisticated managers and entrepreneurs. Quality control was variable and some customers, for example, the Ordnance, were more demanding than others. There were particular problems for barrel proof, the testing of a barrel with a higher-than-usual proof gunpowder charge to check that it was safe. Lower-quality barrels were usually diverted for use in guns for the slave trade. Quality-control concerns ultimately led to the foundation of the Birmingham Proof House in 1813 in order to ensure that Birmingham products were demonstrably safe.

The methods used in Birmingham were primarily craft-based. There was little experimentation in Britain making interchangeable parts for firearms other than some work carried out by the Tipton-born London gunmaker Henry Nock in 1796. Interchangeable manufacturing – making everything exactly the same – was promoted in eighteenth-century France as it allowed damaged weapons to be repaired in the field by using components of one to repair another. Interchangeability required the development of sophisticated powered machines and gauging systems and ultimately a simpler ignition method – the percussion cap rather than the flintlock.

Mechanisation and the interchangeable system did arrive in Birmingham but not until the 1860s with the founding of the Birmingham Small Arms Company. It is perhaps fortunate that the Birmingham trade did not take this approach until it

© David Williams/Vince Scothern

did. If this had happened during the Napoleonic Wars Britain may not have been able to make the guns it needed for the war effort. Birmingham's approach was essentially mass manufacture without machines, using many workers and diverse skills.

A war of numbers

It has been estimated that between 1804 and 1815 the Birmingham and Black Country trade made 1.75 million military weapons, 3 million military barrels and 2.9 million gunlocks, together with an estimated million guns for the East India Company and half a million sporting guns. The success of the delivery of 1.6 million military India Pattern Brown Besses, the workhorse weapon for Britain and some of its allies, was achieved by a carefully organised contract made in 1804 by the Ordnance with 11 gunmakers, 18 barrel makers, 20 lock makers, 7 bayonet makers and 11 rammer makers at a price of £1 14s 1d for each musket and bayonet. The peak year of production was 1813 with almost 280,000 being made – the high point of the industry at this time. Ketland and Allport were the second-largest contractor for India Patterns, the largest being another Ketland partnership, Ketland and Walker. Muskets were inspected at Government View rooms built in Birmingham in 1797 and shipped by

canal to the new Royal Military Depot at Weedon Bec in Northamptonshire, which had been founded by Act of Parliament in 1803 'for the service of His Majesty's Ordnance', and thence to where they were needed.

After the Napoleonic Wars were over there was a reduced demand for military supplies and the West Midlands economy slipped into recession.

However, it is clear that the gun trade was one of Birmingham's most important industries during this period, and that it had a global impact – on military conflicts, civilian life, the slave trade, and the subsequent growth of the British Empire.

David Williams is Professor of Healthcare Engineering at Loughborough University. His personal research examines the early years of the Birmingham Gun Trade and its competitors.

Further reading:
Richard Holmes, *Redcoat. The British Soldier in the Age of Horse and Musket* (Harper Collins, 2001).
David Williams, 'James Farmer and Samuel Galton, The Reality of Gun Making for the Board of Ordnance in the Mid-18th Century', *Arms and Armour*, 7: 2, 2010, pp. 119-41.
David Williams, *The Birmingham Gun Trade* (History Press, 2009).
Visit the Birmingham Gun-Barrel Proof House at www.gunproof.com for more about its 200 years of history.

Further background on the Birmingham Gun Trade can be found at www.birminghamgunmuseum.com.

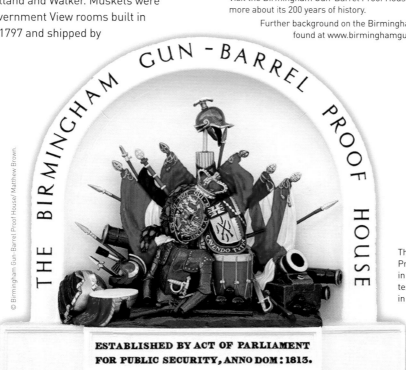

The Birmingham Gun-Barrel Proof House was established in 1813 by Act of Parliament to test the quality of guns made in the town.

LIEUTENANT JOHN VANDELEUR OF WORCESTER

Andrew Bamford

John Vandeleur of Worcester, who fought at Waterloo with the 12th Light Dragoons, began the day of 18 June as a spectator to the battle of Waterloo. He ended it as a hero, after seeking out and rescuing his commanding officer, left for dead on the field.

The charge of the 12th Light Dragoons at Waterloo. John Vandeleur rescued his commanding officer, left for dead on the field, after the regiment's engagement with French infantry. Detail from watercolour by Richard Simkin.

John Vandeleur of Worcester was in many ways typical of the sort of young man filling the junior commissioned ranks of Wellington's army. The Vandeleur family was an Irish one, and John's father was one of three brothers, all of whom had served as army officers. Of the three, one had fallen victim to illness and the other had been killed in action in India, whilst John's father – also John – had risen to command a cavalry regiment before being obliged to leave the service due to the poor state of his health.

With his wife and growing family, he had retired to Barbourne, on the outskirts of Worcester. The family finances appear to have been less than robust, for although there was money enough to keep up a house and to set five sons on their way in life, there was none to spare to allow John and the two younger brothers who followed him into the Army to purchase their way through the ranks.

What is more, John's letters home contain frequent pleas for financial assistance, often being addressed to his mother and asking her to intercede with his father in the hope of a loosening of the purse strings. Those letters, privately published in 1894, give us a useful insight into John Vandeleur's experience of military service between 1810 and 1815, including his participation in the Battle of Waterloo.

Reproduced with kind permission of the 9th/12th Royal Lancers Regimental Museum, Derby

Lt. John Vandeleur in later life. An early photograph taken following his retirement from the Army in 1846.

Early action
Although there was insufficient money to purchase a first commission for John Vandeleur, the fact that his father was a retired officer gave him the opportunity of a place as a Gentleman Cadet at the Royal Military College at Marlow. Upon graduation in 1809, aged sixteen, he was appointed as an ensign in the 71st Highland Light Infantry, which he joined the following year: just in time to accompany the regiment's first battalion when it embarked for Portugal to join Wellington's army in its defence of Lisbon.

During the coming months, Vandeleur received a practical education in soldiering to complement the theoretical instruction he had received at Marlow. His letters indicate that he took some time to get used to the hardships of campaign, and was frequently homesick, but that he quickly matured into a good officer.

In spring 1811, having successfully held Lisbon, Wellington began a series of operations designed to drive the French from Portugal. These were largely successful, but the French under Marshal Massena soon mounted a counter-attack which culminated in the three-day Battle of Fuentes de Oñoro. During the course of the fighting the 71st were heavily engaged and John Vandeleur was severely wounded and invalided home.

A coveted commission
It took Vandeleur over a year of convalescence to become fit to return to active service. During this time he first received a promotion to lieutenant in the 71st – which he was due by seniority – and then a transfer, in his new rank, to the 12th Light Dragoons. Obtaining this posting without charge was quite a coup, for cavalry commissions were valued more highly than equivalent posts in the infantry.

Re-equipped and wearing the blue uniform of Britain's light cavalry, Vandeleur returned to the Peninsula in late summer 1812. His initial duties were as a regimental officer, in which role he fought at Vitoria in 1813, but for the last months of the Peninsular War he was assigned to the staff of a distant cousin, Major General John Ormsby Vandeleur, who commanded the brigade of which the 12th were a part.

John Vandeleur remained an aide to the general until his regiment returned to Britain in 1814, and when war broke out again the following year he again sought to serve as a staff officer. Permission was not forthcoming, however, and so his experience of the Waterloo campaign would be as a regimental officer.

The 12th at Waterloo

The 12th were commanded in 1815 by Colonel the Hon. Frederick Ponsonby, a dashing and popular commander who had served with distinction throughout the Peninsular War. Along with the 11th and 16th Light Dragoons they formed part of the Fourth Cavalry Brigade under their old Peninsular chief, and Vandeleur's relation, Major General John Ormsby Vandeleur.

Being stationed well to the rear, west of Brussels, the Fourth Cavalry Brigade missed the earliest fighting of the campaign, arriving at Quatre Bras on the evening of 16 June just as the struggle there was coming to an end. The following day the three regiments helped cover the allied retreat. Writing home, Vandeleur reported that the French 'followed us and skirmished the whole way until we arrived at our position at Waterloo'. Upon reaching Wellington's chosen battlefield, Vandeleur and his comrades spent a wet night bivouacking amidst the standing corn and waiting the resumption of fighting.

From spectator to hero

Posted on the allied far-left, the 12th were not initially engaged on 18 June and Vandeleur was left a spectator to the battle. In the early afternoon, however, the 12th and 16th Light Dragoons were called upon to charge in order to cover the retreat of the British heavy cavalry, which had in turn helped repulse the first major French infantry attack. Engaged with French infantry and

cavalry, the 12th were badly cut up and Colonel Ponsonby was left for dead on the field. Vandeleur survived this stage of the fighting unscathed, but later had his horse shot from under him as the survivors of the regiment moved to reinforce Wellington's right wing in the final stages of the battle.

It was dark before the 12th could stand down, but rather than sleeping Vandeleur went in search of his missing commanding officer. Ponsonby was thought dead, and Vandeleur was warned that he stood little chance of finding one body amidst the fallen, but he went anyway, and at length discovered the colonel 'desperately wounded, piked thro' the body and his arm broken by a sabre cut'. Vandeleur helped him off the field, and Ponsonby eventually made a complete recovery.

In the aftermath of the battle, Vandeleur finally got his desired appointment as aide to his relative the General, and served in that role to the end of the campaign. He remained in the peacetime army, eventually retiring in 1846 after having risen to the command of the 10th Hussars. His military career served to sever the connection with Worcester, and upon starting a family of his own he returned to his ancestral home of Ireland, but it was Worcester that he called home throughout the Napoleonic Wars, and his memories of its people and places pepper his letters throughout this dramatic episode in his life.

Andrew Bamford is a military historian and the author of several books on the Napoleonic Wars, including *Sickness, Suffering and the Sword: The British Regiment on Campaign* (1808-1815) (University of Oklahoma Press, 2013).

Further reading:
Andrew Bamford, *With Wellington's Outposts: The Peninsular and Waterloo Letters of John Vandeleur* (Frontline Books, 2015).

Andrew Bamford, *Gallantry and Discipline: The 12th Light Dragoons at War with Wellington* (Frontline Books, 2014).

Ian Fletcher, *Galloping at Everything. The British Cavalry in the Peninsular War and at Waterloo 1808-15. A Reappraisal* (Spelmount, 1999).

Captain William Hay, *Reminiscences 1808-1815 Under Wellington* (Simpkin, Marshal, Hamilton, Kent, & Co., 1901).

BIRMINGHAM SWORDS ON THE BATTLEFIELDS

Paul Wilcock

Some of the finest swords made in Britain during the late-eighteenth and early-nineteenth century originated in Birmingham. Many of these weapons were carried onto the battlefields of Europe during the Napoleonic Wars, and evidence of their beautiful craftsmanship can still be seen today.

Swords & Pistols Ltd.

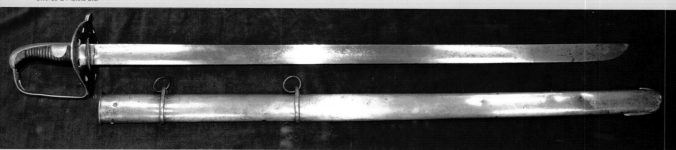

Birmingham produced many of the weapons that defeated Napoleon. This heavy cavalry sword was manufactured by prominent suppliers Osborn & Gunby and is marked to the Scots Greys.

On Sunday 18 June 1815 the nations of Europe gathered on a waterlogged battlefield nine miles south of Brussels to perform the final act of the 23-year drama that was to become known as the Napoleonic Wars. Almost three hundred thousand heavily armed men would decide the fate of Europe. For some their lives would depend upon the effectiveness of their swords, and many of the finest were manufactured and refined in Birmingham.

The British cavalry were equipped with the 1796 pattern cavalry sabre. The version for light cavalry had a murderous curved slashing blade. The heavy cavalry of the Union Brigade were armed with the 35-inch straight steel pallasch based upon the Austrian pattern 1769/75 sabre. The light cavalry sabre had been the creation of Major General John Gaspard Le Marchant and was developed in collaboration with Henry Osborn, sword cutler of Birmingham.

Le Marchant, a highly talented cavalry commander, had fought in the Flanders Campaign in 1793 and had concluded that the swords carried by the British cavalry in particular were significantly inferior to those of the enemy. The design and manufacturing skills of Osborn, combined with Le Marchant's field experience, caused the 1796 light cavalry sword to be proposed and adopted. In 1796, Henry Osborn successfully tendered to supply three thousand of both heavy and light cavalry patterns at a cost of seventeen shillings each. Le Marchant continued to be the leading exponent of military strategy of his time and was killed leading a cavalry charge at the Battle of Salamanca in 1812.

Osborn was born in 1756 and baptised in St Philip's Church Birmingham on 17 December that year. Doubtless the association with Le Marchant was a distinct benefit and Henry continued to maximise his advantage; moving to Bordesley Mills in around 1800 he opened premises in

The heavy cavalry sword immortalised in Lady Butler's famous painting of the Royal Scots Greys at their charge at Waterloo. *Scotland For Ever!* 1881 by Lady Butler.

Pall Mall with significant royal patronage. In 1807 Osborn established a partnership with John Gunby in Birmingham which was to last thirteen years. In that time they produced significant quantities of weapons. The heavy cavalry swords for which they were responsible included the 1796 Heavy Cavalry sword marked to the 2nd North British Dragoons (Scots Greys), the regiment immortalised in Lady Butler's famous painting of their charge at Waterloo.

In addition to fulfilling large commercial orders, Osborn also produced swords such as an officer's sabre of the 1796 pattern with a beautifully etched blade and signed by Osborn in 1798.

From swords to bayonets
The Birmingham sword trade had become well-established by the late eighteenth century, developing a mutually supportive relationship with the gun trade. Osborn and Gunby, for example, also held contracts for

the supply of gun locks to the Board of Ordnance and several of the patents granted to Osborn concerned improvements in gun barrels.

There were many other prominent Birmingham sword manufacturers whose names frequently appear on weapons from the Napoleonic Wars: Craven established a business in Moor Street; Dawes trading in Snowhill; Gill at Masshouse Lane and the partnership of Reddell and Bate worked from premises at Carey's Court. One of the most prolific manufacturers was James Woolley who began manufacturing in 1785 and established the partnership of Woolley and Deakin at Edmund Street in 1800. Swords from the Waterloo period are frequently encountered bearing Woolley's name and contracts with the Board of Ordnance bear out the production not only of swords but also of bayonets.

The reputation of the Birmingham sword cutlers was challenging the high-prestige London dealers with some success. Not only was Birmingham supplying the military in significant quantities, they were also addressing the prestige market. At Drumlanrig Castle in Dumfries and Galloway is a pair of 1796 light cavalry officer's sabres, with fine cut steel hilts, scabbards etched and polished to their full length and blades, etched and then treated in a furnace to prevent corrosion before being gilded and inscribed. They were presentation pieces to the Duke of Buccleuch and Queensberry and to his son the Earl of Dalkeith in 1800 on their respective appointments as Colonels of Militia Regiments. These are some of the finest examples in existence and commissioned, not from one of the premier London cutlers, but from Messrs Woolley and Deakin of Birmingham.

Waterloo swords

The Birmingham sword industry supplied significant quantities of the weapons used to defeat Napoleon in his final stand at Waterloo. With the exception of swords in museums or in private collections with provenance to an individual soldier, they are today more difficult to identify with any certainty.

One sword, however, may come close. Josiah Reddell and Thomas Bate had worked independently as sword cutlers and are also recorded in partnership at Dale End from 1803. The sword is signed by Bate on the blade and bears the

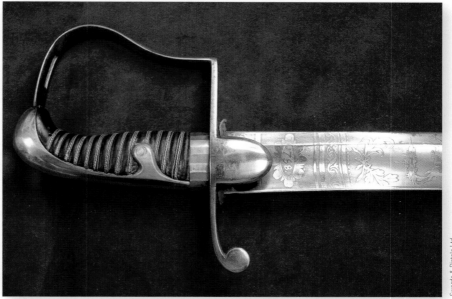

As well as swords in numbers, Henry Osborn supplied officer's sabres with beautifully-etched blades.

cartouche of Reddell and Bate on the scabbard. The blade also carries the Board of Ordnance acceptance stamp. German customs records identify imports of light cavalry swords into Prussia in both 1807 and 1813, totalling sixteen thousand. These were used to re-equip the Prussian forces, particularly the *Landwehr* regiments, in their fight against Napoleon. A particularly fascinating aspect of this sword is the Prussian regimental marking and the contemporary repair to the scabbard shoe in the Prussian style. The markings certainly identify the squadron and sword number (3E – 3rd Squadron sword number 275). The marking on the crossguard, 8LR, may indicate the initial issue to the 8th *Landwehr* Regiment.

Whether or not the sword itself entered the fray on 18 June 1815 will never be known for sure. What is certain is that it began life in Birmingham in the workshops of one of the country's most respected sword manufacturers. It was then purchased by the Crown, exported to Prussia, and played a role in the campaign to free Europe from French Imperial domination, before eventually returning to England to become the property of a private collector.

Reverend Paul Wilcock BEM is Director, Arms and Armour Research Institute, University of Huddersfield.

Further reading:
Richard Dellar, *The British Cavalry Sword 1788-1912: Some New Perspectives* (The British Cavalry Sword, 2013).

Brian Robson, *Swords of the British Army. The Regulation Patterns 1788-1914* (Naval and Military Press and National Army Museum, 2011).

R.H.Thoumine, *Scientific Soldier: A Life of General Le Marchant 1766-1812* (Oxford University Press, 1968).

GENERAL ROWLAND HILL OF SHROPSHIRE

Nick Lipscombe

Rowland Hill joined his first regiment in 1790 and forged his military career in the French Revolutionary and Napoleonic Wars. He was Wellington's most trusted subordinate, a consummate soldier and a compassionate leader.

Rowland Hill (1772-1842) was born to a well-established Shropshire land-owning family whose ancestors had amassed considerable wealth and property as traders during the reign of Henry VIII and had subsequently occupied senior positions under William III and Queen Anne. Rowland was the second son, and fourth child, of 16 children born to John Hill and Mary Chambre. Rowland and his brothers and sisters had an idyllic childhood; the Hill children were 'familiar with the River Severn, the farms, the grain fields and cattle, and the numerous mines located in the region'. Educated at Chester he was earmarked for a career in law. Rowland, however, had no such plans, making clear his intention to follow his elder brother's footsteps and pursue a military career. Somewhat bemused, but aware of Rowland's wishes, his father purchased him an ensigncy in the 38th (Staffordshire) Foot. Hill joined his Regiment in July 1790.

French Revolutionary Wars

The following year he took up a lieutenancy in the 53rd (Shropshire) Regiment. In 1793 he volunteered for action

From a wealthy Shropshire family, Rowland Hill was one of Wellington's most trusted commanders. *Lieutenant-General Rowland, Lord Hill*, 1819 by George Dawe.

The National Army Museum/Mary Evans Picture Library.

at the siege of Toulon and it was here that he met Thomas Graham (later Lord Lyndoch) who became a lifelong friend. In 1794 Graham raised the 90th Foot (Perthshire Light Infantry) and invited Hill to join him, on the proviso that Hill recruited large numbers of men from his native Shropshire. In 1796 the 90th Foot deployed to Gibraltar and by 1800 Hill was in command of the Regiment, taking part in the Battle of Alexandria the following year.

Master strategist of the Peninsular War

He had to wait until the outbreak of the war in Iberia before seeing action again, by which time he was a Major General. He commanded a brigade under Wellesley (the future Duke of Wellington) at Vimeiro in August 1808 and another in Moore's army which fought a desperate rearguard at Coruña in January 1809 before embarking on the waiting transports. When Wellesley returned to Portugal with Britain's expeditionary army in 1809, Hill once again received command of a brigade and during the operation to liberate Oporto from Marshal Soult's grasp he was given the first of his many independent missions. It was an early

Rowland Hill at Wellington's side. Pictured to the right of Wellington (centre), this image also includes Henry Paget (far right), another of Wellington's distinguished generals. *Portraits of the General Officers*, pub. H. Colburn, engr. Rouse, 1816.

indication of Wellington's confidence and trust. Within months he was commanding the 2nd Division, but he underestimated French intentions on the eve of the Battle of Talavera when a surprise night attack caught him unprepared. His rapid deployment of his reserve recaptured the position and recovered the situation. Wellington's trust was repaid in 1810 when Hill, deployed in an independent position to the south, made best speed over difficult terrain to join Wellington's army at the ridge of Buçaco.

From 1811 until the end of the war, Hill was, in every sense, an independent commander of a corps-sized force. Four particular actions stand out as beacons of his military prowess. The first, in 1811, which resulted in the dispersion and capture of the French force at Arroyo dos Molinos, was masterful in the speed and surprise with which it was conducted. In 1812 his daring raid on the French-held, strategically important bridge at Almaraz, by way of a precursor to the Salamanca campaign, was equally exceptional. In 1813 at the battle of Vitoria his corps opened proceedings on the allied right flank, securing the Heights of Puebla, but his greatest achievement was at the Battle of Saint-Pierre d'Irube in December 1813 when he held off more than 30,000 French troops with fewer than half that number until reinforced. Hill exposed himself repeatedly at the most dangerous parts of the line, encouraging the defenders with his infectious resolve. At Waterloo Hill was given command of the 2nd Corps and he led the charge of Sir Frederick Adam's Brigade in the last critical stages of the battle.

A compassionate figure

Hill never married. He became a General in 1825, and was appointed Commander-in-Chief of the Army in 1828. He was appointed Governor of Plymouth in 1830 and became Viscount Hill of Almaraz in 1842. He died at Hardwicke Grange, Shropshire on 10 December 1842 and is buried in the churchyard at Hadnall. A 40-metre high column was erected in his honour outside the Shirehall (the Shropshire Council offices); the first stone was laid by the Salopian Lodge of Freemasons in 1814 and it was completed on 18 June 1816, the first anniversary of the Battle of Waterloo.

Rowland Hill was, without doubt, Wellington's most trusted subordinate. He was innovative, bold and utterly trustworthy but it was his extraordinary compassion towards the rank and file which earned him the sobriquet 'Daddy Hill'. Having served the majority of his career in the shadow of the Iron Duke the opportunities to demonstrate the full extent of his martial prowess were curtailed. It is with some irony, therefore, that Hill is remembered more for his benevolence than his soldierly competence. Yet he possessed abundant quantities of the latter.

Nick Lipscombe is a Napoleonic Historian and Tour Guide. He spent 34 years in the British Army. Published work includes his award-winning *The Peninsular War Atlas* (Osprey Publishing, 2nd edn., 2014), *Wellington's Guns: The Untold Story of Wellington and his Artillery in the Peninsula and at Waterloo* (Osprey Publishing, 2013), *Wellington's Forgotten Front* (Gerrard Books, 2013), *Bayonne and Toulouse 1813-14, Wellington Invades France* (Osprey Publishing, 2014) and, most recently, *Waterloo – The Decisive Victory* (Osprey Publishing, 2014).

Further reading:
Joanna Hill, *Wellington's Right Hand: Rowland, Viscount Hill* (The History Press, 2011).

Gordon Teffeteller, *The Surpriser: Life of Rowland, Lord Hill* (University of Delaware Press, 1983).

FIELD MARSHAL HENRY WILLIAM PAGET OF STAFFORDSHIRE

Nick Lipscombe

Field Marshal Henry Paget was one of the most distinguished cavalry generals of the Napoleonic Wars. After campaigning in Spain in 1808, Paget returned to England, where his subsequent affair with the wife of Wellington's younger brother scandalised society. Waterloo enabled Paget to restore his reputation, but also cost him his leg and his military career.

© *Lieutenant General Henry William Paget (1768-1854) c. 1815 (oil on canvas), Stroehling, Peter Eduard (1768-1826)/National Army Museum, London/Bridgeman Images*

Henry Paget, the cavalry general whose distinguished military career was brought to an end by injury at the Battle of Waterloo. *Lieutenant General Henry William Paget (1768-1854), c.* 1815 by Peter Eduard Stroehling.

Henry was born in London on 17 May 1768, the son of Henry Bayly and Jane (*née* Champagné). The following year the family fortunes changed dramatically when Henry senior inherited a baronetcy and succeeded to the title of the 9th Lord Paget of Beaudesert. The new family seat was on the southern edge of Cannock Chase in Staffordshire but the family's good fortune was not to end there for, in 1780, they inherited large tracts of mining land in both England and Ireland. The young Henry Paget was to benefit from the family's new-found affluence; he attended Westminster School and Christchurch College, Oxford.

In 1790, on completion of his studies, he became the Member of Parliament for Carnarvon, but Paget was set on a military career. In 1793, at the outbreak of the French Revolutionary Wars, he raised the 80th Foot (Staffordshire Volunteers) from his father's estates and funding. As a militia lieutenant colonel he commanded the regiment from the outset and took part in the 1794 Flanders Campaign. The next six years were a whirlwind of activity. In 1795 he was formally commissioned into the British Army as a lieutenant in the 7th Foot; almost immediately he gained a captaincy in the 23rd Foot; in early May that was increased to enable him to become a major in the 65th Foot before, on 30 May, he regained lieutenant colonelcy of the 80th Foot.

A month later he transferred to the 16th Light Dragoons. If that was not enough to keep him busy, he also married Lady Caroline Elizabeth Villiers in July 1795.

In 1796 Paget switched parliamentary seats and became Member of Parliament for Milborne Port, Somerset, received promotion to colonel and assumed command of the 7th Light Dragoons the following year. In 1799 he took the regiment to Holland as part of Sir Ralph Abercromby's Anglo-Russian force which failed to remove the occupying French; nevertheless, Paget's talents had been noted.

© Lichfield Camera Club

Appointed Lord Lieutenant of Staffordshire in 1849, Henry Paget is buried at Lichfield Cathedral with his Staffordshire ancestors.

Daring missions in Spain

Paget did not experience military operations again until 1808, by which time he was a lieutenant general. He commanded the cavalry in Sir John Moore's army and fought two actions in December 1808 at Sahagún and Benavente in Spain, during the early stages of the army's harrowing retreat in the face of Napoleon's pursuing corps. The action at Sahagún, handled directly by Paget, was audacious in the extreme and the first triumph for the British cavalry in the war. However, on his return to England Paget's close liaison with Lady Charlotte Cadogan, the wife of the Duke of Wellington's younger brother Henry Wellesley, became too public, making it impossible for Paget to return to the Peninsula and serve with Wellington. Instead Paget was given command of an infantry division which participated in the ill-fated Walcheren expedition. On return he divorced his wife Lady Caroline and married the recently divorced Lady Charlotte. However, the affair was too much for Regency society and damaged Paget's reputation as well as causing considerable ill-feeling and distress with his eight children.

A reputation regained, a career lost

On his father's death in 1812 Paget inherited the title the Earl of Uxbridge. In 1815 he was given command of the British cavalry in Wellington's Anglo-Dutch Army. His initial meeting with the Commander-in-Chief was cold but

Wellington showed no apparent animosity. Uxbridge's command of the retreat from Quatre Bras on 17 June, in conjunction with the horse artillery, was masterfully executed. During the Battle of Waterloo the next day he launched and led, perhaps too intimately given his position, the heavy cavalry brigades, which checked the attack by the Comte d'Erlon, commander of the French I Corps, at a critical juncture. In the dying stages of the epic confrontation Uxbridge was injured by a shell splinter while saddled a few yards from Wellington. By God, sir, I've lost my leg!' he exclaimed in a rather matter-of-fact way, to which Wellington replied, equally impassive, 'By God, sir, so you have!' His right knee was shattered, necessitating amputation. It brought an end to his military career.

A month after Waterloo, 'One-Leg' as he became known, was awarded the title Marquess of Anglesey in recognition of his achievements and promoted to full General in 1819 and Field Marshal in 1846. He continued to serve in public office as Master General of the Ordnance (1827-1828 and 1846-1852) and Lord Lieutenant of Ireland (1828-1829 and 1830-1833). He was appointed Lord Lieutenant of Staffordshire in 1849. He died of a stroke at Uxbridge House on 29 April 1854 and was buried at Lichfield Cathedral. The Cathedral houses a monument and on the Isle of Anglesey a 27-metre column was erected to his heroism. Both are fitting memorials to one of Britain's greatest cavalry generals.

Nick Lipscombe is a Napoleonic Historian and Tour Guide. He spent 34 years in the British Army. Published work includes his award-winning *The Peninsular War Atlas* (Osprey Publishing, 2nd edn., 2014), *Wellington's Guns: The Untold Story of Wellington and his Artillery in the Peninsula and at Waterloo* (Osprey Publishing, 2013), *Wellington's Forgotten Front* (Gerrard Books, 2013), *Bayonne and Toulouse 1813-14, Wellington Invades France* (Osprey Publishing, 2014) and, most recently, *Waterloo – The Decisive Victory* (Osprey Publishing, 2014).

Further reading:
Ian Fletcher, *Galloping at Everything: The British Cavalry in the Peninsular War and at Waterloo 1808-15* (Stackpole Books, 2001).
George Charles Henry Victor Paget, Marquess of Anglesey, *One-Leg: Life and Letters of Henry William Paget* (Jonathan Cape, 1961).

NEWS FROM THE BATTLEFIELD
Waterloo and the West Midlands Press

Andrew Watts

Newspapers enabled West Midlanders to read of Wellington's victory at Waterloo, in the words of the Duke himself. Throughout the nineteenth century, the local press continued to print stories and anecdotes relating to the battle, as well as encouraging the public to commemorate this historic event. Today, Waterloo is still making news.

'The enemy ... fled in the utmost confusion.' Soldiers pore over the Waterloo Despatch, reprinted in a special edition of *The London Gazette* and later in Midlands papers. *The Chelsea Pensioners Reading the Waterloo Despatch*, 1822 by Sir David Wilkie.

C aked in dirt from the battlefield, the Duke of Wellington sat at his desk in the early hours of 19 June 1815 to prepare his account of the allied victory at Waterloo. In his report to Lord Bathurst, the Secretary of State for War and the Colonies, Wellington described how his army had stood firm in the face of numerous cavalry charges and repeated bombardment from French artillery.

He praised the bravery of his men as they fought to defend the farms of Hougoumont and La Haye Sainte, two of the key strategic positions in the battle. And with factual simplicity, he recalled the moment when Napoleon's resistance was finally broken. 'The enemy was forced from his positions on the heights', wrote the Duke, 'and fled in the utmost confusion.'

Wellington's despatch reached Britain on 21 June, and over the days that followed appeared in newspapers throughout the country. First to break the news of the victory was *The London Gazette Extraordinary*, which published the Waterloo Despatch – as this document subsequently became known – on 22 June. As copies of London newspapers began to arrive in Birmingham, a large crowd gathered outside the Hen and Chickens Hotel in New Street – the arrival and departure point for the town's mail coaches – to hear of Napoleon's final defeat.

Since no daily newspapers were printed in Birmingham at this time, it was not until Monday 26 June that *Aris's Birmingham Gazette* featured the Waterloo Despatch. Across the wider region, the *Staffordshire Advertiser* and the *Warwick and Warwickshire General Advertiser* – two newspapers that in this instance had the good fortune to appear

With no daily newspapers printed in Birmingham at the time of Waterloo, The Hen and Chickens Hotel in New Street saw large crowds gather for the arrival of the London papers by mail coach. *Hen and Chickens, New Street* from *Old and New Birmingham*, Robert Dent, 1880.

on Saturdays – were able to publish Wellington's historic statement even sooner, on 24 June. Newspapers enabled the British public to hear and read for themselves the first official account of the battle, sparking joyous celebrations, but also plunging many families into mourning.

Battlefield legends

For the press, Waterloo provided much more than a single newsflash moment. It was an event that spawned countless stories and legends which journalists would delight in recounting for years afterwards. This was certainly true in the West Midlands, where newspapers and periodicals continued to publish Waterloo-related anecdotes – some more truthful than others – throughout the nineteenth century.

One of the more unusual, and indeed macabre, of these stories appeared in the *Coventry Herald* in 1824 and concerned the death of a Sergeant Weir, who served with the Scots Greys. As pay-sergeant for his regiment, Weir collected money from the men for clothes and supplies, a responsibility that normally would have excused him from active combat. At Waterloo, however, he requested permission to charge with his fellow cavalry officers. Weir's sense of comradeship cost him his life, yet according to the *Herald*, he did not succumb to his injuries without first writing his name on his forehead in his own blood, thus proving to those who found his body that he had not simply disappeared with the regiment's money.

While the story of Sergeant Weir retained the attention of the local press only briefly, there were other tales of Waterloo that West Midlands newspapers never tired of retelling.

One of the most intriguing of these stories centred on a Birmingham button seller who reportedly strayed onto the battlefield during the midst of the fighting. In 1892, the *Lichfield Mercury* claimed that Wellington had seen this stranger riding between the fires, and beckoned him over to ask what he was doing there. The button seller replied that he had been on business in Brussels but was curious to witness a battle first-hand.

Impressed by the succinctness of the man's answers, and running short of aides-de-camp, Wellington asked whether he would be willing to take a message across the field to Marshal Kempt, commander of the 8th British Brigade. In the version of the tale published by the *Birmingham Daily Post* in 1872, the Duke told his senior officers to 'have faith in Brummagem' before settling down to doze under a copy of the *Sun* newspaper. When he awoke a few minutes later and saw that Kempt had changed his tactics, Wellington realised that the button seller's mission had been a success, prompting him to exclaim 'Well done, Buttons!'

Whether the story of the Birmingham button seller has any basis in truth is open to question. In what is generally considered an improbable epilogue to the tale, the *Lichfield Mercury* reported that Wellington later summoned the button seller to his home in London, and that in recognition of his good service, the man was

A Glorious Victory.

LONDON, JUNE 22, 1815.

OUR illustrious WELLINGTON has adorned his brow with a wreath of brighter laurel, and diffused a more brilliant ray upon the pages of his country's glory. We will not venture into a detail of the "pride, pomp, and circumstance" of the mighty conflict, as it would be an injury done to the gallant hero, to abridge his own succinct and modest statement. Suffice it to say, that, after a continued battle of four days, the desperate assault of the French, commanded by BONAPARTE in person, was completely repulsed, and the discomfited remains of the beaten army retreated into their own country, leaving *the field covered with their dead*, and TWO HUNDRED and TEN PIECES of CANNON, with a LARGE QUANTITY of BAGGAGE, and TWO EAGLES, as trophies, in the hands of their conquerors!

Such a Victory, under such peculiar circumstances, could not be purchased without a severe loss. The dispatches state it as "immense," and the gloomy catalogue by which it is accompanied, proves too well the truth of the assertion. Some of the best and bravest of our Generals and other Officers have fallen, or have been so severely wounded, as to deprive the army of their valuable assistance at this momentous crisis; and perhaps, when the enthusiasm of the moment—when the flush of triumph will have subsided—it may be calmly asked, whether it has not been dearly purchased? As yet we have no account whether the enemy have lost any of their principal Generals; the dispatches are silent on that head, but it is probable that they have suffered in that respect not less considerably than ourselves.—The particulars of this glorious victory were this day given in a *Gazette Extraordinary*, a copy of which we subjoin·

Across the region, people heard about Wellington's famous victory through reports in local newspapers. *Warwick and Warwickshire General Advertiser*, 24 June, 1815.

rewarded with a post in the Royal Mint at £800 per year. The Duke would have been well placed to secure such a favourable appointment, not least because his older brother, William Wellesley, was Master of the Royal Mint from 1814-1823.

At £800 per year, however, the button seller would have been paid more than even the Chief Engraver, who during the same period received an annual salary of £500. A legend that the West Midlands press did much to popularise, the story of the Birmingham button seller has long proved impossible to substantiate, and the identity of the man himself – if he ever existed at all – remains a mystery.

Commemorating Waterloo

As well as seeking to entertain readers with tales of bravery and daring, local newspapers gave extensive coverage during the nineteenth century to the commemoration of Waterloo. In June 1830, *Aris's Birmingham Gazette* reported on a dinner held in Warwick to mark the fifteenth anniversary of the battle and attended by dignitaries from the surrounding area. In a separate event in the town, members of the Royal Veteran Society also marched to St Nicholas's Church, accompanied by a band of the 5th Dragoon Guards from Coventry which attracted 'an immense crowd'.

Would you take a Message of Importance for me? (engraving), English School, (20th century)/Private Collection/ © Look and Learn/Bridgeman Images.

" 'Would you take a message of importance for me ? ' "

'Well done, Buttons!' Whether fact or fiction, the legend of the Birmingham button seller who carried a message for Wellington found its way into a number of Midlands papers.

As newspapers from this period illustrate, remembrance of Waterloo was by no means a purely solemn activity. Wellington's victory was also an event to be celebrated, and the regional press encouraged readers to enjoy reliving the famous battle in a variety of ways. In March 1835, *Aris's Birmingham Gazette* carried an advertisement for a play based on the Battle of Waterloo at the Theatre Royal in New Street, promising 'new and superb scenery'.

In 1834, the *Birmingham Daily Press* also drew the attention of readers to the Waterloo re-enactment staged by Ryan's Royal Circus in Bradford Street, Digbeth, where the performance included a cavalry charge by the circus's equestrian company and a final ceremony in which the actors dressed as British soldiers were crowned with laurel wreaths. And for those who preferred to remember Waterloo in a less dramatic setting, the *Birmingham Journal* advised the public of the opportunity to visit – for the admission price of one shilling – Captain William Siborne's scale model of the battle, which was displayed in the town in 1840.

The last veterans

As the nineteenth century entered its final two decades, some newspapers in the West Midlands showed a keen interest in the lives and gradual disappearance of the last Waterloo veterans. As the local press clearly recognised, living memories were fading rapidly into history, and risked being lost forever.

The desire to capture such recollections appears to have been the primary motivation behind a long article published by the *Birmingham Daily Post* in October 1887, which focused on the experiences of former soldier John Tyrer (also known as John Taylor). By then aged 96, Tyrer had returned to his native Birmingham after the end of the Napoleonic Wars. Still in robust health, he was described by the newspaper as living 'in peaceful enjoyment of that small pension which, by way of ending the scandal of these old fellows dying in work houses, the War Office granted in 1870'.

Casting his mind back to Waterloo, Tyrer admitted that his company had landed at Ostend on 21 June, three days after the fighting had ended. However, he and his comrades were able to join Marshal Blücher's troops on their victorious march to Paris, and were billeted for a night in the country home of one of Napoleon's generals, Marshal Soult, only to find that it had already been ransacked. The company eventually reached the British camp at Saint-Denis, on the outskirts of Paris, where Tyrer saw Wellington ride daily through the seven-mile stretch of tents to check on his men.

While this eye-witness account of the immediate aftermath of Waterloo was undoubtedly precious, the newspaper was no less eager to record Tyrer's 'reminiscences of old Birmingham'. The veteran duly shared his childhood memories of riots at the Bull Ring over the price of bread, and of witnessing a public hanging at Washwood Heath. He also recalled with sadness the economic slump that gripped the town after the Napoleonic Wars, when 'there were no guns or swords to be made, and hundreds of people had to face starvation'.

The old soldier had lived through a tumultuous period in history, and the decision to interview him for the press ultimately proved to have been timely. John Tyrer would not reach his ninety-seventh birthday, and died on 27 May 1888.

The centenary of Waterloo

By the time of the centenary of Waterloo in 1915, Britain was once again at war. The First World War had broken out in July 1914, and as the country became increasingly preoccupied with events in Belgium and France, marking the anniversary of Waterloo was hardly a national priority.

In the West Midlands, press coverage of the centenary was muted. In Birmingham, the *Evening Despatch* reminded readers of the anniversary of the ball held in Brussels by the Duchess of Richmond on 15 June 1815, at which Wellington received word of Napoleon's advance on Quatre Bras. In more sombre terms, the same newspaper used the example of Waterloo to highlight the terrible carnage of the First World War.

A short, poignant paragraph under the heading 'historic anniversaries' observed that 'contemporary accounts of the Battle of Waterloo read strangely, with their 6,932 British killed and wounded, in the week in which we have learned that our casualties in the present war are already over 258,000. All our standards of comparison are shattered'.

Even in this dark hour of conflict, however, the local press showed that it had not lost its sense of humour entirely. On 12 May 1915, the *Evening Despatch* carried an advertisement for an indigestion remedy called Mother Seigel's Syrup, which stretched the credulity of the most gullible reader by attributing Napoleon's defeat at Waterloo to the fact that he was a dyspeptic. 'At a time when the fate of an empire hung on his initiative and energy,' read the advertisement, 'they failed him. In your own case good health is just as necessary. Indigestion should not be allowed to undermine your strength.'

Still making news

As we approach the bicentenary of Waterloo, local media interest in the battle shows no signs of diminishing. In 2009, the *Birmingham Mail* reported on the auction of a pistol that had belonged to John Waters, a Royal Marine from Shenstone who served on the HMS *Bellerophon*, the ship which took Napoleon into British captivity following his surrender in July 1815. The 16cm pistol was authenticated by the Armouries at the Tower of London and its value estimated at £600. Ahead of the auction, a spokesman for Hansons Auctioneers told the *Mail*: 'Such historical context of the pistol adds romance and mystery to an item which witnessed a great battle.'

More recently still, West Midlands newspapers have helped to reveal some of the personal stories which lead back to Waterloo. In February 2011, the *Birmingham Post* conducted an interview with Linda Atterbury, a grandmother from Erdington whose burgeoning interest in family history – inspired partly by the television series 'Who Do You Think You Are?' – enabled her to discover that her great-great-grandfather, John Fletcher, was present at Waterloo with the 79th Regiment of Foot. 'To go back generations past and find out you had ancestors who were in the military and who fought in battles, like Waterloo – it's absolutely fascinating,' Mrs Atterbury told the newspaper. 'I really feel as though I haven't done anything with my life compared with what my ancestors have done.'

As stories such as these show, the battle continues to fascinate both the local press and its readers. Waterloo is still making news today, just as it did in the wake of Wellington's famous despatch in 1815.

Dr Andrew Watts is Lecturer in French Studies at the University of Birmingham.

Further reading:
David Chandler, *Waterloo and the Hundred Days* (Osprey, 1980).
Paul O'Keeffe, *Waterloo: The Aftermath* (Bodley Head, 2014).
The British Newspaper Archive at www.britishnewspaperarchive.co.uk. This is a subscription service.
A small selection of regional newspapers from 1815, including the *Staffordshire Advertiser* and the *Warwick and Warwickshire General Advertiser*, are held in Archives & Heritage at the Library of Birmingham and can be consulted by appointment.

NAPOLEON ON ST HELENA
A Shropshire Regiment Stands Guard

Guy Sjögren

The 2nd Battalion of the 53rd (Shropshire) Regiment of Foot was appointed in July 1815 to begin a two-year tour of duty preventing Napoleon's escape from St Helena. The former Emperor manipulated his captors as unwitting pawns in his relentless game of divide and conquer against the island's Governor, but ultimately came to hold them in high esteem.

Four months after the Battle of Waterloo, guarded by the 53rd (Shropshire) Regiment of Foot, Napoleon began his exile on St Helena. *Napoleon at St Helena*, L. Kratke, 1894.

On that 'vast mass of rock rising abruptly from the Atlantic Ocean' Napoleon occupied Longwood, the Governor's summer residence.
View and Plan of Longwood House, St. Helena, the residence of Napoleon Bonaparte, 1817. Rudolph Ackermann (publisher).

'How far is St Helena from the field of Waterloo?'
A near way – a clear way – the ship will take you soon
A pleasant place for gentlemen with little left to do.
(Morning never tries you till the afternoon!)

from Rudyard Kipling, *A St Helena Lullaby*

As dawn broke on the morning of 28 July 1815 a King's Messenger clattered into Portsmouth. Secure in the galloper's saddlebag was an order from the Commander-in-Chief addressed to Colonel Sir George Bingham, the commanding officer of the 2nd Battalion 53rd (Shropshire) Regiment of Foot, then stationed in the naval town. The order directed the 53rd to prepare for 'immediate embarkation for distant

service'. At 11 o'clock the battalion formed up for inspection, 'when every man appeared under arms and in complete marching order'.

In view of the dramatic events of the previous fortnight, there seemed little doubt that the 'distant service' was to be on the South Atlantic island of St Helena. And so it was that, some ten weeks later, the battalion disembarked from two troopships lying off Jamestown and were ferried ashore. Thus began a two-year tour of duty, the sole objective of which was to ensure that Napoleon remained secure in his remote island prison. It also marked the beginning of an unusual and fraught triangular relationship between captive, gaolers and 'higher authority' in the form of the British government and the island's Governor.

The 'Old Five and Threepennies'

The 53rd Foot had been raised as a single battalion in 1755. However, at the turn of the nineteenth century, the imperial and wartime involvement of the British Army necessitated its expansion, as a result of which a second battalion of the 53rd was formed in 1803. The First Battalion deployed to India two years later, leaving the Second to fight its way through Spain during the Peninsular War. By the summer of 1815, the 2nd-53rd was back in England.

The Shropshire Regiment's archives hold a document which states: 'The result of the Battle of Waterloo, having deprived Bonaparte of all powers, induced him to adopt the determination of delivering himself to the British government.' This is not quite true. Napoleon's original aim was to escape to the United States, one option being to smuggle him out of Rochefort hidden in a barrel aboard a Danish vessel carrying a cargo of brandy. However, the Royal Navy's blockade of the port made this impossible and, on 15 July, Napoleon boarded HMS *Bellerophon*, declaring to the captain: 'Sir, I am come to throw myself upon the protection of your Prince and of your laws.'

Protection he was certainly given, but not in the way that he wanted. Stripped of his imperial title, Napoleon was henceforth referred to as 'General Bonaparte'; and, rather than living a quiet life in England as he had hoped, he was dispatched to what the naval surgeon assigned to him described as 'a vast mass of rock rising abruptly from the Atlantic Ocean...jagged and irregular, cut and slashed, as it were, cut into pieces by the great hatchet of nature'.

© Anne S.K. Brown Military Collection, Brown University Library.

Sir Hudson Lowe, Governor of St Helena and his prisoner taunt each other. *Hudson Lowe: Oui général, c'est un bien petit royaume pour un grand homme comme vous! Napoleon: Heureusement, c'est tout le contraire pour vous, Sir Lowe! (Hudson Lowe: Yes, General, it's quite a small kingdom for a great man like you! Napoleon: I'm happy to say that it's quite the opposite for you, Sir Lowe!)*

Three days of feverish activity followed the arrival of the King's Messenger in Portsmouth, and on 1 August the battalion began to embark on the troopships *Bucephalus* and *Ceylon* anchored off Spithead. The troopships arrived in Tor Bay on 6 August where, by now, the *Bellerophon* was waiting. Napoleon was then transferred to HMS *Northumberland* and, early that evening, the *Northumberland*, the troopships and escorts, under the command of Admiral Sir George Cockburn, weighed anchor and headed out into the English Channel.

Exile to St Helena

There is little doubt that Napoleon's departure from Europe was met with relief in many quarters. The *Morning Post* of 3 August argued that, while he had lost physical power, he still possessed a moral power, and that 'to give him his liberty would enable him to disturb the repose of the world'. Four days later, the same newspaper was in even less conciliatory mood, referring to Napoleon as 'this wretch' and an 'inhuman tyrant'. It would take some ten weeks and a 'boisterous passage' for the squadron to reach St Helena and deliver its 'obnoxious charge' (the *Morning Post* again) ashore.

While permanent accommodation was being prepared for Napoleon at Longwood – hitherto the Governor's summer residence – Napoleon spent his first two months on the island living in a small pavilion adjacent to 'The Briars', the home of William Balcombe of the Honourable East India Company. There, and with Cockburn as Governor, he seems to have been reasonably content. All was to change, however, with his removal to Longwood in December 1815 and the arrival of General Sir Hudson Lowe as Governor the following April.

Napoleon caricatured employing his military skills with the legions of rats to be found on St Helena. *War in the East against the Cats, by Napoleon the Great, of St. Helena.* Thomas Rowlandson and Rudolph Ackermann, February 23, 1816.

Lowe has received a bad press. He has been described as unimaginative, unbending and over-zealous in his treatment of the former Emperor; even Wellington thought him the wrong man for the job. And yet Lowe bore the almost overwhelming responsibility of applying the government's regulations, the sole objective of which was to prevent Napoleon from escaping, as he had done from Elba the previous year. But if Lowe considered Napoleon a prisoner, the former Emperor did not. Even when aboard the *Bellerophon*, Napoleon had remonstrated: 'Tell the Prince Regent that I have one thing to ask, my liberty or an executioner. I am not the prisoner of England.' Protest as he might, he was clearly treated as such.

A naval exclusion zone was thrown around the island, whilst on land Napoleon's movements were constrained. Longwood sat on a plateau 1,800 feet above sea level and his movements were restricted to an area around Longwood some twelve miles in circumference.

The 'Shropshire lads' of the 2nd-53rd were camped a mile away at Deadwood Plain. Soldiers patrolled the plateau, manned temporary outposts, or *picquets*, placed at intervals around the perimeter, and acted as sentries in the immediate vicinity of Longwood. Living at Longwood was Captain Thomas Poppleton, the senior captain of the 53rd assigned as Napoleon's orderly officer.

Napoleon sympathised with the lot of the 53rd, occupied as they were with largely passive duties. 'I have no reason to complain about them', he said, 'they treat me with respect, and even appear to feel for me.' When not on guard duty, the soldiers were constantly formed into fatigue parties.

Everything required at Longwood and Deadwood had to be laboriously manhandled up from the town – even water, as there was none on the plateau. In Napoleon's opinion, it would have been better to have dedicated resources 'in conducting water to those poor soldiers in camp than throw up fortifications round the house, just as if an army were coming to attack it'.

Divide and conquer

In view of the tight military security surrounding Napoleon, it was clearly impractical for him to consider escaping from St Helena. On the other hand, like any prisoner of war, he refused to accept his situation, and to this end he employed all his well-honed political and strategic skills: skills he had used to keep the loyalty of his army and the support of the people. If he could not make a physical escape from the island, he would find an alternative way of gaining his liberty. His strategy brought him deliberately into constant conflict with the Governor. It also involved him in playing a game of divide and conquer; a game in which he would use elements of the 53rd as unwitting pawns.

Napoleon recognised that his only hope of getting off the island was to generate sympathy from his supporters in France, as well as sympathetic liberals in England. He realised that if he submitted to Lowe and the regulations, he would be forgotten by the public – out of sight, out of mind. Thus through intermediaries, smuggled correspondence and meetings with travelling visitors, he would complain about his treatment: a lack of decent food, insufficient wine, inadequate supplies of hay for the horses, the living conditions at Longwood, and the rats. 'The rats are in numbers almost incredible at Longwood', wrote Barry O'Meara, Napoleon's doctor. The 53rd's camp at Deadwood was equally infested and, in his memoirs, O'Meara describes a rat hunt led by Captain Poppleton.

One of the restrictions that particularly irked Napoleon was the need to be accompanied by Poppleton whenever he went riding. 'Not that I have any objection to Poppleton', he said, 'I love a good soldier of any nation.' On one occasion, Napoleon suddenly turned his horse and galloped up a steep slope. Unable to follow him, Poppleton hurried off to the Governor. 'Sir, I have lost the Emperor!' he reported, only to be told to go back to Longwood where he found Napoleon at lunch.

Whilst the former Emperor may have had fun at Poppleton's expense, he also appears to have regarded the officer with some affection. Nevertheless, he also used him for his own purposes. Lowe was furious on learning that Napoleon had borrowed a case or two of

claret from Poppleton, and that the latter had 'often lent candles, as well as bread, butter, poultry and even salt'. Equally, it would not have pleased Lowe to know that Napoleon held his 'red regiment', as he referred to the 53rd, in high esteem. 'They are a regiment of brave men and have fought valiantly.' Lowe would also not have cared for Napoleon's 'high approbation' to have been referred to by Lord Bathurst, Secretary of State for War and the Colonies, in the House of Lords.

'Adieu, mon ami'

When, in July 1817, the time came for the 53rd to be relieved as guard regiment, Napoleon asked that the officers be allowed to wait upon him. The regimental archives note that: 'After wishing them every happiness and prosperity, he thanked them for the attention and respect he had always experienced.' He then presented Poppleton with a gold snuff box, saying: *'Adieu, mon ami, voilà la seule bagatelle que me reste'* (Farewell, my friend; this is the one trinket I have left). Lowe was not so generous and, suspecting that Poppleton was carrying home secret papers from Napoleon, set a charge against him. Bathurst, however, rejected it. This was to be the final twist in the brief triangular relationship between Lowe, Napoleon and the 'Old Five and Threepennies'.

Guy Sjögren is a doctoral research student at the Centre for West Midlands History, the University of Birmingham.

Further reading:
Lucia Elizabeth Abell, *Napoleon and Betsy: Recollections of Napoleon on St Helena*, edited by Alan Sutton (Fonthill, 2012).
Paul F. Brunyee, *Napoleon's Britons and the St Helena Decision* (The History Press, 2009).
Brian Unwin, *Terrible Exile: The Last Days of Napoleon on St Helena* (Tauris, 2010).
La Fondation Napoléon at www.napoleon.org.
Further information on the 53rd (Shropshire) Regiment of Foot can be accessed online via www.shropshireregimentalmuseum.co.uk.

WELLINGTON AND WATERLOO IN COMMEMORATIVE CERAMICS

Miranda Goodby

The Napoleonic Wars spawned a prolific industry in commemorative ceramics and other artefacts. While manufacturers often sought to mock Napoleon, they also afforded a special place to the Duke of Wellington, depicting him both as the hero of Waterloo and later as a distinguished politician and national leader.

'Up guards and at them'. The Duke of Wellington on his bay horse, Copenhagen, pointing towards the enemy. Possibly produced to mark the Duke's death in 1852, the figure was still in production a century later.

Up guards and at them.

The early nineteenth century saw British potters producing a wide variety of commemorative ceramics. Jugs, bowls, teapots, figures and plaques were all produced to ridicule Napoleon, mourn the death of Nelson, celebrate victories or short-lived peace treaties, and encourage patriotism in the face of threatened invasion.

By the time of Waterloo the British had been fighting the French for over twenty years, firstly in the Revolutionary Wars, and then after the failed Peace of Amiens, in the Napoleonic Wars. The successes of Wellington and his generals in the Peninsula were widely celebrated at the time, but curiously very few pottery commemoratives can be firmly shown to have been made specifically to mark this particular victory.

Arthur Wellesley, Duke of Wellington (1769-1852), was during his lifetime the subject of many commemorative tributes in pottery, prints and other materials. A large number were made during the Napoleonic Wars while others were produced during his later career as a politician, Prime Minister and Commander-in-Chief of the British Army. Many of the later commemorative pieces refer back to Waterloo.

Wellington's successes in the Peninsula Campaign had led to him being ennobled in 1809 and he became an increasingly popular hero at home. In response the potters produced a variety of commemorative pieces, mostly printed or moulded jugs. These can often be dated by the inscription showing the name of the battle or the title that Wellington bears.

Wellington commemoratives and the Potteries

In the collection of the Potteries Museum & Art Gallery, Stoke-on-Trent, there are a number of pieces commemorating Wellington and his victories. The majority are unmarked and the pottery firms that produced them are unknown. The potters would have used the inexpensive popular prints that were widely available from specialist print shops or stationers as the source of their designs and in some instances these sources can be closely dated.

One such piece, a pearlware jug, bears a printed and enamelled image of a mounted Wellington, urging on his troops with the battle raging in the background. This subject was taken from an engraving of Wellington at the Battle of Salamanca, published in 1812. The same image was re-used by the potters the following year, suitably titled, to commemorate the victory at Vitoria. Thereafter it was used, either untitled, simply inscribed with the word 'Wellington', or titled 'Marquis Wellington in the Field of

Inexpensive popular prints were widely used by potters as a source for their designs. Although this image originally depicted Wellington at the Battle of Salamanca, it was turned to use again on this pearlware jug to commemorate victory at Waterloo.

Reverse of the pearlware jug depicts Bonaparte escaping the Russians carried on the back of a French soldier.

Battle' - and therefore suitable to commemorate the next of the General's victories.

This print was also the source of the design of a moulded and painted jug. One side depicts Wellington as shown in the print of 1812, and the other shows military trophies, including weapons, flags and drums. This example also bears the owner's monogram and the date: 'WN 1815'.

Another popular subject, known in various sizes, was a moulded jug with boldly coloured bust portraits of both Wellington and General Hill. Wellington is described as 'Marquess' on the majority of these jugs but Hill is always 'General Hill' which must date their initial production to between 1812 and 1814.

These pieces would have been relatively inexpensive: mass-produced in earthenware and comparatively crudely coloured, they were made to record events at the time and could be reissued quickly each time there was a demand for images of the victorious generals.

More expensive pieces were also produced. The Staffordshire firm of Wood & Caldwell reproduced, in enamelled earthenware, the marble bust of Wellington originally produced by the sculptor Joseph Nollekens in 1813. The majority of these reproductions bear the mark of Wood & Caldwell, whose partnership ended in 1818. However, some examples date from the 1820s, when they were produced by Enoch Wood & Sons, the firm which succeeded Wood & Caldwell. These life-size busts were aimed at a very different market from the mass-produced, cheaply coloured jugs and were intended for middle-class consumers.

A political figure

Wellington's long career as a politician and, from 1842 until his death, as Commander-in-Chief of the British Army meant that many other commemorative pieces were produced. Many show him in civilian dress, as a politician, or as a very aged man, but others show him on horseback as the victor of Waterloo.

In 1824 Astley's Amphitheatre in London produced a spectacular re-enactment of the battle with over one hundred horses. It was revived at times throughout the nineteenth century and may have contributed to the popularity of the equestrian figures of Wellington. The song 'Buy my Images' published in 1842, and supposed to be sung by an Italian 'image seller', refers to these figures:

> *"Look a dis Images dis nex' one*
> *Capitano Generale de LORD WELLINGTON*
> *Him fight Buonoparte beat him too*
> *And make fas' run 'way from Waterloo.*
> *Great as a Roman was he to de foes*
> *Every bodys knows him well by's nose*
> *Every body trues what every body says*
> *De greatest man living alive dis days.*
> *Buy my Images!*

One of the most widely known equestrian figures shows the Duke on his bay horse, Copenhagen, pointing forward towards the enemy and titled 'Up guards and at them'. Despite the subject matter this figure was not produced until the mid-nineteenth century. Although unmarked, it is believed to be by the Burslem-based factory of Thomas Parr. This firm was in operation from around 1852-1870 and this subject was probably produced to mark the death of the Duke in 1852. Thomas Parr's pottery – and his moulds – changed hands and were acquired by the firm of William Kent, which continued producing figures until 1962. These later figures showed the Duke, incorrectly, on a white horse and were available from the manufacturer at 53 shillings per dozen in the late 1930s. Such was the enduring interest in Wellington and Waterloo that this figure was in production by William Kent until at least 1955. For more than a century after the Napoleonic Wars, the potteries of Stoke-on-Trent continued to draw steady income from the popularity of these commemorative pieces, which today serve as a precious record of this defining period in British history.

Miranda Goodby is Senior Curator of Ceramics at The Potteries Museum & Art Gallery, Stoke-on-Trent.

Further reading:
The website of The Potteries Museum & Art Gallery can be found by visiting Stoke-on-Trent Museums at www.stokemuseums.org.uk.

REMEMBERING WATERLOO IN THE REGIONAL LANDSCAPE

Chris Upton

The Battle of Waterloo was one of Churchill's 'punctuation marks in history', significant not only for bringing to an end twenty-two years of European war, but for its profound impact upon the map of the Continent. Local manufacturers were quick to capitalise upon the event, but it also left some more surprising legacies in the region.

'A felicitously preserved moated manor'. Brinsop Court, Herefordshire, bought by David Ricardo in 1817. Ricardo fuelled and then profited from shareholder uncertainty over the outcome of the Battle of Waterloo.

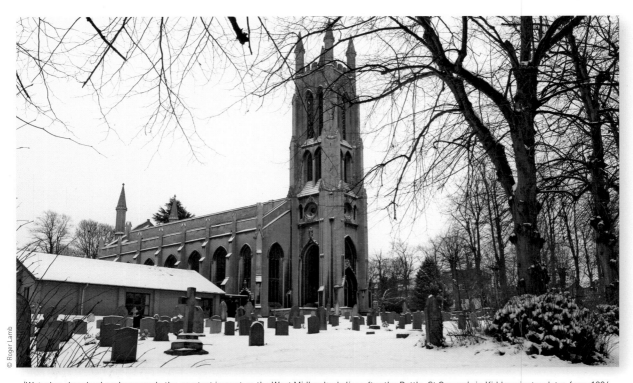

© Roger Lamb

'Waterloo churches' perhaps made the greatest impact on the West Midlands skyline after the Battle. St George's in Kidderminster dates from 1824.

The importance of the Battle of Waterloo was not lost on the manufacturers of the West Midlands, who found immediately lucrative ways to celebrate the outcome. At Bilston they made enamel boxes, decorated with images of Marshal Blücher, the Prussian general. The pottery firms of Staffordshire produced figurines of Wellington, as well as souvenir plates, while the Birmingham ballad-makers dashed off newly minted songs to celebrate the demise of 'Boney'.

But the battle had a longer legacy than this, seen in many surprising ways. Let us take, perhaps, the most extreme of examples: a large hole in the ground in Hockley and a stately home in Herefordshire.

Depression leaves its mark

The post-1815 years marked one of the worst depressions in British economic history, as the government attempted to claw back the national debt, and trade and manufacture spiralled downwards. That impact was felt acutely in Birmingham, when the European market for its goods began to dry up. With unprecedented levels of unemployment and a workhouse full to overflowing, the Birmingham overseers were forced to introduce labour schemes to find work for its jobless men.

One of those schemes carved out a permanent marker on the Jewellery Quarter, where applicants for relief were paid three-farthings a barrow to dig sand out of the Hockley sand mines and wheel it to the canal. Digging continued for more than twenty years, creating two cavernous excavations, which now form the central feature of the cemeteries at Key Hill and Warstone Lane. It is most clearly visible at the catacombs of the Anglican cemetery. Not everyone, however, found their lifestyle pinched.

Brinsop Court

Brinsop Court is one of Herefordshire's finest houses, six or so miles north-west of the county town. Pevsner describes it as 'a felicitously preserved moated manor', set in its own secluded valley. First built in the thirteenth century, the house and its 800 acres were purchased in 1817 by David Ricardo. Ricardo was one of the leading classical economists of his age, his theory of 'comparative national advantage' forged in the years of Napoleonic turmoil. Ricardo made his fortune from stockbroking, and was not above rigging the market to his advantage. One particularly lucrative punt was on the outcome of the Battle of Waterloo. Ricardo scared shareholders into selling British stock, in the mistaken belief that Wellington would lose, and then bought them at a knock-down price.

By such means Ricardo turned his modest income into a fortune, which funded a land grab worthy of Napoleon himself.

Written in the streets

Waterloo is written through the fabric of our region, and the victory over Napoleon ushered in a string of street and house names across the nation. Across the West Midlands there are more than twenty streets named in commemoration either of Waterloo or the Duke of Wellington, a figure which could be greatly increased by widening the map. In Burslem there is Waterloo Road (completed in 1817), and in the Ivy House area of Hanley is Waterloo Street, Wellington Street and Wellington Terrace.

Waterloo Street in central Birmingham was at the heart of the Pemberton estate, while Wellington Road formed a cornerstone of the development of the Calthorpe estate in Edgbaston. Waterloo Road in Kings Heath, though created much later, takes its name from a farm built shortly after the battle. The Dukes of Cleveland cut Waterloo Road in the 1820s to open up their estate in Wolverhampton, while Waterloo Road in Smethwick provided a similar spinal cord to the expanding town. The marvellous Waterloo Hotel nearby (an Edwardian building, high on the 'at risk' register) takes its name from the road, rather than from the battle itself.

And in those many Wellington Roads it is not uncommon also to find an Apsley House, named in honour of the Iron Duke's London residence. Wellington Road in Edgbaston boasts one such, as does Wellington Street in Cradley Heath.

Churches, but no statues

What is absent in the West Midlands are memorials to the Duke, in striking contrast to the rest of the country. Perhaps Wellington's later political career, and his steadfast resistance to Reform, diluted or expunged any

lasting gratitude for his military exploits in our region. Perhaps the greatest impact of the battle upon the West Midlands was on its skyline, and the so-called 'Waterloo churches', funded as an act of thanksgiving by the government in 1818. St Thomas, Bath Row, was one such church, though a later European war has reduced it to little more than a tower. More striking and complete is St George's in Kidderminster, finished in 1824.

Local stories

Waterloo, then, left its mark, and no more so than in the stories it left behind, which only grew with the telling and the passage of time.

The artist, Benjamin Robert Haydon, it would appear, first tells the tale of the Birmingham button seller, who made an excursion from Brussels to Waterloo as a tourist, having never experienced a battle before. Wellington added his unexpected encounter with the man to his catalogue of after-dinner stories.

If doubts have been raised about that tale, so have they concerning the memorable exchange between the Duke and Henry William Paget.

At the exact moment of victory, almost the last volley of enemy grape-shot lashed into Paget who was riding close by the Duke of Wellington. 'By God, sir,' exclaimed Paget, 'I've lost my leg!' 'By God, sir,' replied the Duke, 'so you have !'

What is certainly true, however, is that Paget's famous leg, interred near the battlefield, became a tourist attraction in its own right, while the rest of him rose to become Marquess of Anglesey, with a family seat at Plas Newydd.

On his death, however, Paget chose interment beside his Staffordshire ancestors in Lichfield Cathedral. Having had one foot in the grave for almost forty years, the brave Marquess now had both.

Dr Chris Upton is Reader in Public History at Newman University, Birmingham.

Further reading:
M. Port, *Six Hundred New Churches: The Church Building Commission 1818-1856* (Spire Books, 2006).
Read more about Bilston enamels on The History of Wolverhampton website at www.wolverhamptonhistory.org.uk by entering 'Bilston enamels' into the search box.
Friends of Key Hill and Warstone Lane Cemeteries at www.fkwc.org.

PLACES TO VISIT

Guy Sjögren

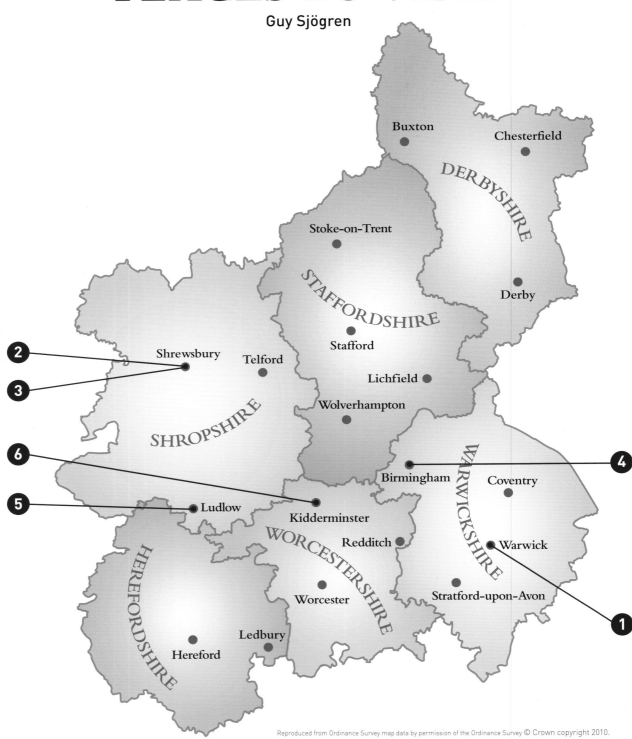

Waterloo in the West Midlands

① The Queen's Own Hussars Museum

Formed in 1689, the 7th (Queen's Own) Hussars was, surprisingly, the only West Midlands regiment to have fought at Waterloo. Drawn from Warwickshire and Worcestershire, this cavalry regiment was one of sixteen such British regiments that formed part of the allied cavalry corps at Waterloo. Although not committed to the battle until late in the afternoon, the 7th Hussars made more than a dozen charges against Napoleon's forces, suffering the highest percentage of casualties of any British cavalry unit. Housing exhibits from the battle and subsequent periods of the regiment's history, the museum is located in the ancient and impressive Lord Leycester Hospital in Warwick - a building worthy of a visit in its own right.

The Queen's Own Hussars Museum,
60 High Street, Warwick CV34 4BH
Phone: + 44 (0)1926 492035
www.qohmuseum.org.uk

③ Lord Hill's Column, Shrewsbury

② The Shropshire Regimental Museum

The 53rd Regiment of Foot was formed in 1755 and was later designated 'The Shropshire Regiment'. Having served in numerous conflicts, the regiment sailed for India in 1805 and remained there for nearly twenty years. However, such was the demand for troops during the early 1800s that a second battalion was formed in 1804. This battalion served with Wellington throughout the Peninsular War but was in England at the time of Waterloo. Following Napoleon's detention, the battalion accompanied him to St Helena where it was to act as his guard until 1817. The Shropshire Regimental Museum, housed in the border fortress of Shrewsbury Castle, is beautifully presented and, amongst other items, contains exhibits relating to the regiment's time on St Helena – including a lock of Napoleon's hair.

Shropshire Regimental Museum, The Castle,
Castle Street, Shrewsbury, SY1 2AT
Phone: + 44 (0)1743 358516
www.shropshireregimentalmuseum.co.uk

As Nick Lipscombe's article suggests, General Lord Hill was one of Wellington's most trusted commanders, both during the Peninsular campaign and at Waterloo. It can also be argued that Hill is Shropshire's most famous soldier. So highly esteemed was he that almost £6,000 was raised by county subscription to pay for a monument in his honour. Completed in 1816, Lord Hill's column, as it is known, stands in an appropriately commanding position at the eastern end of Shrewsbury's Abbey Foregate. The Doric column, surmounted by a statue of the General, is 133 feet in height, and thus exceeds Nelson's Column by some fifteen feet. The elements have not been kind to the statue and plans are afoot to replace it with a replica.

Lord Hill's Column, Abbey Foregate,
Shrewsbury, SY2 6ND
www.friendsoflordhillscolumn.co.uk

4 The Birmingham Gun-Barrel Proof House

© Birmingham Gun-Barrel Proof House

The Birmingham Proof House was established by Act of Parliament in 1813 and was paid for by members of the then prosperous Birmingham gun trade. Its purpose was to provide a testing and certification service for firearms in order to prove their quality of construction. Two hundred years on, the Proof House remains largely unchanged in both purpose and construction. In 2000, a museum was opened at the Proof House with the aim of reflecting the role which the arms and ammunition trades played in the industrial heritage and expansion of Birmingham. Guided tours of the museum can be arranged for groups of between four and ten people. Go to the website below, click on 'Museum' and follow the link to 'Visits'.

The Birmingham Gun-Barrel Proof House,
Banbury Street, Birmingham, B5 5RH
Phone: + 44 (0)121 643 3860
www.gunproof.com

5 Lucien Bonaparte in the West Midlands

© Ron Hoe

Lucien Bonaparte was a younger brother of the more famous Napoleon. Lucien's revolutionary political views led to an abrasive relationship with his older sibling. The brothers eventually fell out over Lucien's marriage, forcing Lucien into self-imposed exile in Rome. In 1809, he attempted to sail to the United States, but his ship was intercepted and he was brought to England. Prisoner as Lucien was, the government allowed him and his family to live comfortably. He spent six months at Dinham House in Ludlow before moving to Thorngrove House in Worcestershire. Thorngrove is not open to the public. However, Dinham House, although currently occupied by Clearview Stoves Ltd, is accessible. The company generously allows individual visitors to wander through the house, where there is a small museum dedicated to Lucien Bonaparte and other occupants of the house.

Dinham House, Dinham, Ludlow, SY8 1EH
Phone: + 44 (0)1584 878100
www.clearviewstoves.com/ludlow

6 The Waterloo Churches

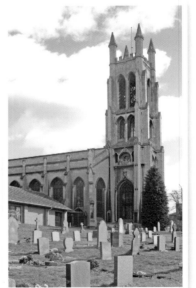

© Mattie Underhill

A combination of an expanding urban population and an inadequate supply of church seats led to the passing of the Church Building Act in 1818: legislation that allocated one million pounds for the construction of new churches. Some of the new churches were known as 'Waterloo churches', and were built in an act of national thanksgiving for the defeat of Napoleon at Waterloo. At least three were built in the West Midlands. Of the two Birmingham churches, St Peter's, Dale End was demolished in 1899, and St Thomas, Bath Row was partially destroyed during an air raid in 1940. However, the church of St George, Kidderminster is still a flourishing parish church and has a commanding position overlooking the town.

St George's Church, Radford Avenue, Kidderminster, DY10 2ES
Phone: + 44 (0)1562 822131
www.kidderminstereast.org.uk